# *NO SWEAT* ELEVATOR SPEECH!

# ***NO SWEAT***
# ELEVATOR SPEECH!

How to Craft **YOUR**
Elevator Speech Floor by Floor
with **No Sweat!**

FRED E. MILLER

***NO SWEAT*** *Elevator Speech!*

Copyright ©2021, 2014 FredCo.

All rights reserved, including the right of reproduction in whole or in part in any form. No part of this book may be reproduced in any form without written permission of the publisher.

ISBN 978-0-9843967-1-9
1. Public Speaking   2. Presentations   3. Business

Cover illustration and design copyright © 2021 by FredCo.

Book interior design by Patrick Dorsey.
Interior art by Charles Manion © 2014 by Charles Manion.
Cover design by Ken Joy.
Edited by Deb Gaut.

Typeset in Ebrima and Hit The Road.

First edition published 2014.
Third edition 2021.

Manufactured in the United States of America.

NoSweatPublicSpeaking.com

To order additional copies of this book, contact the author at **NoSweatPublicSpeaking.com/contact/**

# Dedication

This book is dedicated to everyone, *including me,* who has struggled with their Elevator Speech.

It's for all who stammer, sweat, and generally embarrass themselves when answering the question:

> *"Who are you and What do you do?"*

*Don't give up!*

This book holds the answer.

Read it—Study it—Practice it.

And *your* Elevator Speech will be absolutely, positively—

*NO SWEAT!*

# Contents

Acknowledgements ................................................................ vii

Introduction ............................................................................ xi
    Your Elevator Speech Is Outstanding–*Isn't It?* ................ xi
    "*Speaking* Opportunities are *Business*, *Career*, and *Leadership* Opportunities!" ........................................... xii

**Chapter 1—The Elevator Speech** .......................................... 1
    The Really Quick, Short, and B-o-r-i-n-g Ones .................. 4
    The *Please Sit Down!* Elevator Speeches ........................ 4
    Going Forward, I'm Going to Cover: ................................. 7

**Chapter 2—What is an Elevator Speech and Why Should You Have One?** ........................................................ 9
    Elevator Speech Audiences: Individuals and Groups ....... 11
    Elevator Speech Goals ...................................................... 12
    Elevator Speech Guidelines .............................................. 17
    The Ultimate Elevator Speech Test .................................. 19

**Chapter 3—Developing the *ULTIMATE* Elevator Speech Template** .................................................................. 21
    The Backstory .................................................................. 21
    Two Words Helped to Craft My *ULTIMATE* Elevator Speech Template ................................................................ 23

**Chapter 4—My ULTIMATE Elevator Speech** ....................... 31
    My ULTIMATE Elevator Speech ....................................... 32
    My ULTIMATE Elevator Speech—Floor by Floor ............ 33

Let's Get in the Elevator! .................................................................. 34

**Chapter 5—Three Variations of Your Elevator Speech ...... 55**

Skipping Floors ............................................................................. 55

The *EXPRESS* Elevator Speech ................................................... 56

The Twitter-Type Elevator Speech .............................................. 59

**Chapter 6—The Elevator Speech: Delivering It ................... 61**

Note it–Remember it–Practice it! (The *Magic of Three!*) ....... 63

Nonverbal Communication: Vocal Cues .................................... 64

Enunciation and Pronunciation .................................................. 65

Inflection ....................................................................................... 65

Speech Rate .................................................................................. 66

Pausing .......................................................................................... 68

Volume .......................................................................................... 69

Quality ........................................................................................... 69

Nonword Sounds ......................................................................... 69

Forms of Nonverbal Communication ......................................... 70

Eye Contact .................................................................................. 71

Facial Expressions ........................................................................ 72

Gestures ........................................................................................ 73

Body Language ............................................................................ 75

Posture .......................................................................................... 75

Body Movement .......................................................................... 76

Clothing ......................................................................................... 77

A Final Note about *In*voluntary Nonverbal Communication 78

**Chapter 7—Bonus Tips for a Great Elevator Speech ........ 81**
    Greet People! ................................................................................ 81
    Continually Take the Temperature of Your Audience ........... 82
    Interact with Your Audience ..................................................... 82
    Buzz Words ................................................................................... 83
    Filler Words .................................................................................. 84
    Clichés .......................................................................................... 85
    Taglines ........................................................................................ 87
    Be Conversational ...................................................................... 88
    Quotable Quotes ........................................................................ 88
    The Rule of Three ....................................................................... 89
    Props ............................................................................................. 92
    Practice. Practice. Practice ........................................................ 93

**Chapter 8—Tips for Networking ............................................ 97**
    Find an Event .............................................................................. 97
    Networking Goals ...................................................................... 98
    *Before* the Event–Make a Plan ................................................ 99
    *During* the Event—Work Your Plan ................................... 101
    Delivering Your Elevator Speech One-on-One During the Event ........................................................................................... 104
    Have a Getaway Plan .............................................................. 106
    Delivering Your Elevator Speech to a Group During the Event ........................................................................................... 107
    Develop a *Post*-Networking Event Plan ............................. 108

**Chapter 9—Fear of Public Speaking ................................... 111**
    WHY Do People Fear Public Speaking? ............................... 112

Imposter Syndrome ........................................................................ 112
Fear of Failure ............................................................................... 113
Reasons Behind Our Fear of Public Speaking ....................... 114
Other Factors that Can Bring on Fear of Public Speaking .. 115
What-Ifs? ........................................................................................ 115

## Chapter 10—Nuggets to Lessen Fear of Public Speaking 117

Nervousness ................................................................................. 117
*Never* Tell Your Audience You Are Afraid! ............................ 117
You Don't Have to Be Perfect .................................................. 118
Be Audience-Centered ............................................................... 118
All Audiences Are Not the Same ............................................. 120
Arrive at Events Early So You Can Meet & Greet ................ 121
Find Friendly Faces in Your Audience ................................... 122
Have a "Spare Tire" .................................................................... 123
Deep Breathing Exercises .......................................................... 123
Get a Good Night's Sleep .......................................................... 124
Keep Your Body in Good Physical Condition ...................... 124
Meditation ..................................................................................... 125
Medication, Hypnosis, Psychotherapy, or Tapping ............. 126
Cotton Mouth .............................................................................. 127
Join Toastmasters ........................................................................ 128
Take Courses ................................................................................ 129
Hire a Coach! ............................................................................... 129
Fear Busters .................................................................................. 131
Practice! Practice! Practice! ....................................................... 133
My Golden Nugget! .................................................................... 135

The Real Learning is in the Doing!...................................................136

**Chapter 11—*Failure* Gets a Bad Rap...................................139**

**Chapter 12—Conclusion .......................................................143**

   Goals of an Elevator Speech ...........................................143

   Delivery ................................................................................145

   Close.....................................................................................146

# Acknowledgements

### *Bill Prenatt*

Bill is the founder and dynamic, past leader of Experts for Entrepreneurs (e4e), a high-level networking organization he formed in 2010. I am proud to have been one of the original members.

This book would never have been conceived or written had it not been for Bill "volunteering" me to speak at an e4e meeting about how to develop, practice, and deliver an awesome Elevator Speech with–*NO SWEAT!*

At the time of his "request," my first book titled *NO SWEAT Public Speaking!* had been published. After one e4e event, he told me I'd be the right person to speak about Elevator Speeches. Like many, I had struggled with my own for years, but there was no way I'd refuse anything Bill asked of me. The endeavor took me *way* out of my comfort zone, but, as we know, when we get out of our comfort zones, they become *larger.*

Following that initial "Elevator Speech" talk were many more presentations to a wide variety of groups. I also developed a workshop on the topic and wrote the first edition of this book.

I'll forever be thankful for Bill's "suggestion" to make that presentation.

### *Deb Gaut*

Deb is the consummate editor! It is not an exaggeration to say she helped me transform this book from good to *GREAT!*

*Fred E. Miller*

Just like there was a story about Bill Prenatt that initiated my speaking, writing, and giving workshops about Elevator Speeches, there is a wonderful backstory about how I came to have the privilege to work with Deb Gaut.

I write a regular column for the *St. Louis Small Business Monthly*. The first of each month, when the online version is published, I search for it, find my column, give it a cursory look, and copy the link. I take that link and place it into my social media applications.

One month, I decided to read the published article in its entirety. As I read it, I started thinking, "This is good!"

Further into the column, I told myself, "This is *really* good."

At about the halfway mark of the composition, I realized, *"I didn't write it this good!"*

In the back of my mind, I knew that Ron Ameln, the publisher of *St. Louis Small Business Monthly*, had an editor review articles before publication. Until that point, I had no idea how much value a professional editor could add. I had used editors previously, but mostly for correcting punctuation and spelling errors.

Placing my submitted article next to the published one Deb had edited showed the *little* edits she made that resulted in a *huge* difference in the quality of the final product.

I called Ron to ask who edited my article and if it was normal to be as shocked as I was about how the final product was significantly better than the initial one. He said my experience was not unique and he had hired Deb for editing because she is the *best!*

With that information, it was a no-brainer for me to contact Deb and see if I could engage her editing services. We hit it off immediately and it was one of the best business decisions I've ever made.

Without her help and guidance, which went far beyond punctuation and spelling, this book would not be nearly as good as I know it is.

# Introduction

## Your Elevator Speech Is Outstanding—Isn't It?

You're at a networking event, social function, or seminar and the leader says, "Before we get started let's go around the room. When it's your turn, stand and tell us *WHO* you are and *WHAT* you do. Give us your **Elevator Speech**."

When I was given those instructions, I often started sweating. I sometimes thought about it as a *"religious experience"* because in my mind I found myself invoking phrases like, "*Please!* Don't call on me first. I know I should have been prepared for this. I *will* be ready next time."

When *you* are called upon to deliver *your* Elevator Speech, is it YES or *YIKES?*

If *YIKES* is your response like it was for me, ***this book is for you!***

*Most* people struggle with their Elevator Speeches. I did for years.

Not having and being able to deliver an outstanding Elevator Speech is a problem. It's a problem because...

Fred E. Miller

## "*Speaking* Opportunities are *Business*, *Career*, and *Leadership* Opportunities!"

That's my mantra and no one ever challenges it. *Why would they?*

An **Elevator Speech** is a *mini-Speaking* Opportunity. Are you *taking* and *making* these *mini-Speaking* Opportunities? If not, you're losing out. You're losing out because *the research shows* that people who take and make *Speaking* Opportunities, like delivering great Elevator Speeches, grow their businesses, advance their careers, and increase their leadership opportunities.

In this book I'll explain how to develop, practice, and deliver *outstanding* Elevator Speeches to take and make those *mini-Speaking* Opportunities with–*NO SWEAT!*

At one time I was in a networking group called Experts for Entrepreneurs (e4e). After publishing my first book, "*NO SWEAT* Public Speaking!" Bill Prenatt, our leader, "volunteered" me to deliver a presentation to our members about Elevator Speeches.

*YIKES!* was my reaction. I grappled with my Elevator Speech for years and it was always a 'work in progress.' Developing, practicing, and delivering an Elevator Speech to peers took me *way* out of my comfort zone. In retrospect, it wound up being a *good* thing because I discovered that being out of my comfort zone made it *larger.*

I decided to develop an Elevator Speech template and based it on two words:

*NO SWEAT Elevator Speech!*

1. **Elevator**
   Build it floor by floor.
2. **Speech**
   An Elevator Speech is a mini-presentation.

I researched, studied, and redesigned many Elevator Speech templates. Eventually, after much testing and getting feedback from others, I came up with a very flexible and useful one.

After developing that Elevator Speech Template, I wrote the first edition of this book. It wasn't long after publishing *NO SWEAT Elevator Speech!* that I started reading, learning, and thinking about material I *should* have included. At first it frustrated me. I quickly realized that's how it should be and usually is. "The road to perfection never ends." This book is the culmination of the first edition and the many things I've learned about Elevator Speeches since it was published. I know it could include more material but, as Zig Ziglar said, "If you wait till all the lights are green, you'll never leave home."

This *New* and *Expanded* Edition of *NO SWEAT Elevator Speech!* will show you how to develop, practice, and deliver outstanding Elevator Speeches with–*NO SWEAT!*
If you want to be confident and excited about telling others *WHO* you are and *WHAT* you do—**this book is for you!**

**Let's get started!**

*Fred E. Miller*

# Chapter 1—The Elevator Speech

When I'm addressing an audience about the topic of Elevator Speeches, I open my talk by *raising my hand* and asking, "By a show of hands, who has *changed*, *trashed*, or *tweaked* your **Elevator Speech** within the last year?"

*Immediately,* many hands go up.

I'll continue, "In the last six *weeks?"*

"In the last six *days?"*

*"As I'm speaking, you are?"*

If you're like most attendees who answer this question, you'll raise your hand throughout my questioning, and you'll probably chuckle a bit when I ask the last question.

I struggled with my Elevator Speech for years. It was always a "work in progress." My research shows that most people experience the same challenge, and that's probably one of the reasons you're reading this book, *correct?*

**We've all been there.**

You attend an in-person or online networking event, social function, or seminar, and the leader announces, *"Before we get started,* let's go around and introduce ourselves. When it's your turn, tell us *who* you are and *what* you do. Give us your *Elevator Speech."*

For me, this used to be a *religious moment.* In my head, I'd be saying, *"Please*, don't let the facilitator call on me first. I know I should have been working on my Elevator Speech, and I should have been prepared. I'll be ready next time. *Please* don't let me embarrass myself by being picked first!"

At this point, I am avoiding eye contact with the leader, hoping he or she calls on another attendee or someone jumps up and exclaims, *"I'll go first!"*

I'm sure *you've* never considered doing so, but more than once I've thought about grabbing my phone, pretending I had an important call, and excusing myself from the event.

Ultimately, when someone else starts delivering an Elevator Speech, it feels like a huge weight has been lifted from my shoulders. That comfort doesn't last long because then I start thinking, "What if the person just ahead of me delivers one of those *Killer* Elevator Speeches?" You've heard those speeches– the ones where everyone *Oohs!* and *Ahs!* about how wonderful the presentations are. *That* could be *worse* than being called on first!

Then the Elevator Speeches begin, and as always, the quality of content and delivery are all over the place.

## A Few Great Ones

Occasionally, a few *really* good Elevator Speeches emerge. The speakers get right to the point and tell us

- Their names
- Their companies' names
- Their titles or roles
- The products and/or services they offer
- An item or two about *their* expertise
- Something that distinguishes them *personally* from others in the same roles

**Example:**

"Hi, everyone!

I'm Don. I'm an estate planning attorney. That's the only legal work I do, and I've done it for more than 25 years.

I've written quite a few articles about the topic, which you may have seen in local publications. I've also been interviewed by the media as an authority on estate planning.

Wills, trusts, directives, and more: The laws often change on such legal documents, and I keep abreast of all of them.

If you're thinking about creating an estate plan or want yours to be reviewed to see if it's current and includes *everything* a good plan should have, *let's have a conversation.*"

I'm impressed! Don seems to "know what he's doing" in this specific area of law. He's establishing a *lot* of credibility.

After hearing his Elevator Speech, I can decide if I want to know more. If I do, I'll catch up with him during a break, after the event, or later. If I'm happy with my current plan, I'll mentally file his name should a need arise in the future. I'm also comfortable *referring* him to others if the subject of estate planning comes up in a conversation.

## The Really Quick, Short, and B-o-r-i-n-g Ones

These Elevator Speeches provide minimal information and offer nothing that grabs our attention or interests us enough to want to know more.

**Example:**
"I'm Louise. I'm a bookkeeper. If you need bookkeeping work done, call me."

*Really?* You've told me *nothing* that distinguishes you from your competition or gives me any reason to think you're an expert bookkeeper. *Why* would I want to meet with you? I can't imagine *ever* referring you.

## The *Please Sit Down!* Elevator Speeches

Elevator Speeches in this category either give too little or no pertinent information about the speakers and their products or services, *OR* they go on and on with too much information, a great deal of which is irrelevant.

### The Cutesy Ones That Don't Say Much

These folks think they can "tease" you into "*wanting* to know more about them and their offerings." They are *wrong!*

**Examples:**

"I'm Robin, the Financial Plumber for *All* Your Money Troubles." Work with me, and I'll help you flush those problems out of your life forever!"

## NO SWEAT Elevator Speech!

*or*

"I turn men who are Wall Flowers into Chick Magnets!"

*You've got to be kidding me!* What you said is too vague. I have no idea what either of you do—and have no desire to know more.

Both Elevator Speeches sound like potential con jobs, and I *won't* waste my time finding out more.

### The Long, Long, L-o-n-g Ones

At the other end of the spectrum from the Cutesy Ones are the *Long, Long, L-o-n-g Ones* where individuals ramble on and on and on...

If they offer ten products, they'll tell you about fifteen! Then they'll give several "case studies" about how their products or services forever changed the lives of people or companies making purchases, ignoring "dings" from the timer for the speeches to STOP! *Finally*, they'll sit down! They've left little time for others to present within the time allotted for the exercise, and they've mentioned so many things that you have no idea what they really do.

It's *too* much information, across *too* much time, and *so far* from what an Elevator Speech should be that we're better off not hearing it.

You've experienced such Elevator Speeches, haven't you? They're terrible, and I can't imagine wanting to spend more time with the speakers! If you really were on an elevator with them, you'd be prying the door open to get off or hitting the emergency button!

## *The Business Opportunity Ones*

These people usually want to build "down lines" for their multi-level marketing (MLM) businesses. MLM works well for many people, but *please*, tell us *very clearly* what you do! There may be folks in the room who are looking for these kinds of opportunities, but we're not mind readers.

**Example:**

"I'm Susie, and I went from being $50,000 in debt to making $10,000 a week, and I'll show YOU how to do it, too!"

*Really?* The statement *may* be truthful. If so, let the audience know from the get-go what company helped you accomplish this feat and what products or services you sell.

One of my problems with this type of Elevator Speech is that it doesn't give me a clue what the speaker does for a living. Unfortunately, if you ask the person this question, he or she rarely gives you a direct response. It's usually something like, "Let's set a time and date for coffee, and I'll give you the details. Is next Monday morning at ten o'clock at the downtown Starbucks OK with you?" By this time, they're usually holding a smart phone and hoping to confirm the appointment.

*NO SWEAT Elevator Speech!*

Again, if you're offering a *business opportunity, tell* us in the Elevator Speech. For some in the audience, that opportunity might be a *perfect* fit.

## Going Forward, I'm Going to Cover:

- **Elevator Speeches**
    - *What* are they?
    - *Why* have great ones?
- **Different** *Audiences* **for an Elevator Speech**
- *Ultimate* **Goal** of an Elevator Speech
- *Immediate* **Goals** of an Elevator Speech
- How I Developed the *ULTIMATE* **Elevator Speech Template**
    - It works well for me and will do so for you, too.
- **The Ultimate Elevator Speech**
- **The** *EXPRESS* **Elevator Speech**
- **The 'Twitter-Type' Elevator Speech**
- **How to Deliver an Elevator Speech**
- **Bonus Tips to Take Your Elevator Speech from** *Blah* **to** *Ah!*
- **Fear of Public Speaking**
    - It's a big reason people don't like Elevator Speeches.
        - *Why* we have this fear
        - Nuggets to lessen the fear

# Chapter 2—What is an Elevator Speech and Why Should You Have One?

An Elevator Speech is a personal, mini-infomercial that tells people quickly and clearly *who* you are and *what* you do.

It's one of the most important tools for networking with others to exchange information and develop professional or social contacts. People use Elevator Speeches when looking for

- Prospects for products and services
- New career opportunities
- People who can help them achieve personal and professional goals

**Master Networkers** are individuals who know *making referrals* can be a valuable component of their business.

In his book *Influence*, Robert Cialdini writes about the "Law of Reciprocity." His hypothesis is that by giving to others, you receive more in return than if you're engaging in no giving activities. In other words, if I'm regularly referring prospects to you, the odds are you'll be on the lookout for people who can use my products and services in return.

In *The Go-Giver*, Bob Berg offers a similar theory, expanding it to the universe. He suggests that when I refer business to you, the universe is watching–and *someone other than you* may 'reciprocate' and send me prospects. Great!

Based on these two books, one of my goals is to be *"that person."* If *I* don't know someone who offers what you're looking for, I *know* someone who does.

An Elevator Speech is also used in non-business situations when we meet new people. We're naturally curious about what others do and often exchange such personal information.

"Elevator Speeches" got their name from messages that were short enough to be shared in the time it takes for an elevator ride, usually 60 seconds or less. They're designed to be concise and to the point, and to answer the question, "What do you do?"

I have never delivered an Elevator Speech in an elevator and can't say I know anyone who has. That said, the concept is a great one.

An Elevator Speech is *not* meant to sell your products and services, or yourself for a job. Doing so is definitely unacceptable. In the business world, the Elevator Speech is basically a *sorting* and *sifting* tool.

While seemingly simple, this singular objective is often challenging to achieve.

People who hear your Elevator Speech should know *exactly* what you do.

The Goal of All Communication–verbal, written, or visual–is the same.

We want our listeners to *GET IT!* as quickly as possible!

*Clarity is a must.*

If listeners have a clear understanding of your offerings and believe you have expertise, you can realize your Elevator Speech goals.

## Elevator Speech Audiences: Individuals and Groups

### Individuals (In-Person or Virtual)

We give Elevator Speeches to individuals in both *unplanned* and *planned* settings.

**Unplanned Elevator Speeches** can take place anywhere and anytime we meet new people. We can be standing in line for a movie, concert, or carnival ride, and strike up a conversation with folks around us. Someone introduces himself by saying, "I'm Bob. I work over at Home Depot in the Paint Department. What's *your* name, and what do *you* do?"

We also share unplanned Elevator Speeches when we attend social functions, seminars, and informal gatherings–basically, anywhere people get together.

**Planned Elevator Speeches** take place most often in business settings (e.g., immediately prior to formal events, during breaks in scheduled programming, and after events). Fortunately, we often know about such opportunities in advance via program announcements like this one: "Before our scheduled program at 8 p.m., we have time allotted for networking. Get here by 7:30 p.m. and *network!*"

## Groups

A group can be a handful of people or a large audience, and they can be formal or informal.

I've attended Meetup events with as few as three attendees where we started the event by delivering our Elevator Speeches.

People attending larger gatherings, such as my public speaking class with twenty or more students, often are asked to "stand up and tell us *who* you are, *what* you do, and what you want to get out of this program."

The goals and guidelines for Elevator Speeches are the same for both audiences.

## Elevator Speech Goals

### *Ultimate Goal: A Conversation*

Elevator Speeches in business situations share the same ultimate goal: A *conversation* with someone who has a sincere interest in your products and services for themselves or someone else, and who wants more information.

When your listeners want a conversation, they're looking for **details**.

- How much does your product or service cost?
- What are the terms?
- What discounts are available?
- How long has your product or service been available, and what is the track record?
- How does your offering differ from those of your competitors?

## NO SWEAT Elevator Speech!

- Do you offer a guarantee? If so, what is it?
- How is your product or service delivered?
- Would you be willing to share professional references?
- Other questions specific to their needs

If you're looking for a job, your listeners will be taking note of these details:

- What specific company, companies, or industry are you exploring?
- What is your experience in this or related fields?
- What specific skills do you possess that make you a viable candidate for this line of work?
- What degrees, certifications, and credentials have you attained?
- What awards have you earned?
- What references can they contact?

After that conversation they'll know *exactly* what you do, and they'll make one of three decisions.

- **Now!**
    o They're interested in you and your products or services, and they want to buy now or hire you for a job.
    o Example:
        - You sell tires and mine didn't pass the state inspection. I want to talk to you *now!*
- **Not Now, but Perhaps in the Future**
    o They know what you do, and they don't have a current need. However, because you successfully presented yourself as an expert, they'll feel comfortable contacting you in the future for an extended conversation if a need arises.

- o They're also comfortable referring you to others.
- o Example:
  - You sell tires. My car has about 30,000 miles on my current set and probably should last a few more years. However, if I have a blowout or another tire problem, you're on my short list of people to contact.
- **Referral Only**
  - o They have no current need and foresee no future need for what you do.
  - o They *do* have a clear understanding of your services and will feel comfortable referring you if someone ever mentions an interest in products, services, and expertise such as yours.
  - o Example:
    - You sell tires, but I don't own a car. I bicycle, walk, or take an Uber to go places. Despite my transportation situation, many of my friends and family members do have vehicles. I'm happy to refer you because of my confidence in you after hearing your Elevator Speech.

## *Immediate Goal: Complete Understanding*

You want everyone who hears your Elevator Speech to *immediately* understand *what* you do; *sort and sift* that information; and decide the next step. The choices are:

- Have a conversation now or schedule one.
- They know what you do, don't have an immediate need, but would talk to you in the future and refer you.
- *Dis*-**qualify** themselves.

- There are people who will never need anything you offer.
- They never refer individuals to friends or colleagues.
- Additionally, there are people whom you *don't* want to deal with, now or ever. Be happy they *Dis*-qualify themselves!
- Example:
  - You sell tires, but I was *underwhelmed* by your Elevator Speech. I travel by bus and don't do much socializing or networking.

*Dis*-**qualifying listeners for yourself is particularly important in person-to-person Elevator Speeches.**

As an immediate goal, *Dis*-qualifying your listeners should occur more often than it does in many one-on-one Elevator Speech situations...especially during events in which we're asked to "arrive early and *network.*" There is usually a limited amount of time to talk before a program or meal begins. Make the most of the time by *Dis*-qualifying.

In short, "Don't spend *major* time on *minor* possibilities." If the person you're speaking with has no interest in what you do, find out *sooner* rather than later. If that's the case, move on to another person and continue *Dis*-qualifying.

Everyone is not a prospect for what you offer, and you personally aren't going to buy everything that's offered to you.

**Example:**

I once attended a Chamber of Commerce luncheon with the following preliminary agenda:

11:00   Doors open for registration
        Networking begins

12:00   Lunch

12:30   Business Meeting

1:00    Speaker

1:30    Adjourn

I arrived at 11 a.m., registered, and immediately started networking. I specifically remember meeting a lady who sold replacement windows for older homes. She had a great Elevator Speech, and I was very familiar with the window manufacturer. Her company, the local distributor, had been in business a long time and had a great reputation.

The problem was that she was delivering her great Elevator Speech to *every person* she met.

Many were *not* prospects, now or probably in the future.

- Some lived in apartments.
- Others had newer homes that needed no replacement windows.
- And many, even if they owned an older home, probably didn't have the budget for these windows, which I knew were very expensive.

She was wasting *her* time and *their* time by not quickly *Dis*-qualifying. Because the period for networking was relatively short, she was limiting opportunities to find real prospects for herself and those with whom she was talking.

*NO SWEAT Elevator Speech!*

## Elevator Speech Guidelines

### *Clarity*

*Everyone* who hears your Elevator Speech should have a crystal-clear understanding of what you offer: Products and services, or experience and credentials when seeking a new job.

When you are presenting your products or services, they should be logically related.

**Example:**

"I'm a speaker, coach, and author."

As you'll see in future chapters, these activities are related to a single topic for me—Public Speaking.

Both you and I have heard Elevator Speeches where the speakers go on and on about the many *different* things they do. The products and services they mention seem to share no commonalities. Sometimes the speeches get to the point where you believe the speakers can rotate your tires, change your oil, and wash your windows on the second story of your house!

### *Conciseness*

Remember, the term "Elevator Speech" is derived from the idea of telling someone *who* you are and *what* you do in the span of time it takes for an elevator to move from floor to floor. That ride is *quick* and usually takes less than a minute.

Research shows Less = More.

People want to understand things *now!*

That's why CliffsNotes® and executive summaries are popular.

## *NO Selling!*

Selling–if it occurs at all–will take place in the future. In the minds of listeners, *sorting and sifting* is happening during your Elevator Speech. Decisions are quickly being made to determine if your offering is a fit for them, now, never, or in the future. If and when your listeners have a need for your products and services, they'll want to have a conversation and get more information.

## *Consistency*

Your Elevator Speech should be consistent in content that's well adapted for your particular audience (e.g., corporate executives vs. vendors/suppliers vs. actual users/customers). This statement doesn't mean you can't have a number of different Elevator Speeches for different roles in your life. It *does* mean you want listeners representing a specific group or audience to hear the same message about products and services you offer. Consistency is key to avoiding confusion and clouding your brand.

**Example:**

I coach, speak, and write about networking, public speaking, and presentation skills. I also am skilled at mind mapping. (Mind mapping is a nonlinear, visual, brainstorming tool.) If I include mind mapping in an Elevator Speech for people who are unfamiliar with the term, I can easily confuse my listeners. I do have an Elevator Speech for this expertise and use it when speaking to prospects for that tool.

***NO SWEAT Elevator Speech!***

You can have a different Elevator Speech for your job, club, or volunteer organization. Just remember to keep the content of your Elevator Speech consistent and adapted appropriately for your audience.

## The Ultimate Elevator Speech Test

*Everyone* who hears your Elevator Speech should be able to tell anyone who *hasn't* heard it *exactly* what you do.

In turn, *that* person should be able to share the same information about you.

# Chapter 3—Developing the ULTIMATE Elevator Speech Template

## The Backstory

I've been in Elevator Speech Hell more times than I care to admit. When called upon for my mini-infomercial, I'd get tongue-tied, flustered, and unable to clearly articulate "*who* I am and *what* I do." I struggled with that short speech for years. It was always a *work in progress.* Because you're reading this book, I'll bet *you've* struggled, too.

When someone tells you they don't know what you do after you've delivered an Elevator Speech, it's embarrassing. I've been there.

**I was *Volunteered* to speak about Elevator Speeches.**

I had participated in several networking groups. One of them, Experts for Entrepreneurs, had a dynamic leader, Bill Prenatt. He approached me after one of our monthly events and said, "Fred, you're our public speaking, presentation expert. How about giving our group a presentation next month on how to develop a great Elevator Speech?"

*"Jeez,"* I thought to myself. Mine *stinks*! It's going to be tough to develop a presentation on something I've struggled with for years. *Bummer!*

Bill's request for a presentation on Elevator Speeches was *not* a suggestion. It was my *assignment*. That was OK, because it was something I'd been avoiding and knew I needed to work on. I speak, coach, and write about public speaking and presentation skills. I *should* have a great Elevator Speech and should be able to train others on developing, practicing, and delivering theirs.

I was thankful for the assignment because it got me out of my comfort zone. I know when I get out of my comfort zone it becomes larger–Good!

Confirming to Bill that I would deliver that presentation the following month immediately got me motivated to start working on it. However, I had no idea where to begin.

Luckily, the next day, while sitting in my weekly sales class, something happened that gave me the punch and direction I needed.

We had a new student. Before the lesson started, and as usually happens with a newbie, the instructor announced, "This is Tim's first day. Before we get stated, let's go around the room. When it's your turn, stand and tell him *who* you are and *what* you do. Give him your *Elevator Speech.*"

I blundered through mine as did most of my classmates. However, Roy, who was seated next to me, said something so profound that *everyone* stopped, grabbed a piece of paper, and wrote it down. **One sentence** in his Elevator Speech made it stand out from all the others. **One phrase** in that sentence was *strikingly* different than anything I'd ever heard in an Elevator Speech. Those words sparked a fire in me to develop my ULTIMATE Elevator Speech Template. *Keep reading and I'll tell you what he said!*

## Two Words Helped to Craft My *ULTIMATE* Elevator Speech Template

### *Elevator*

As I said earlier, the term "Elevator Speech" came from the idea of being in an elevator with someone and telling them *who* you are and *what* you do by the time the doors open on the next floor.

One thing about the word **Elevator** jumped out. It goes up or down, **one floor at a time.**

## Boom!

With that concept in mind, I decided to develop my *ULTIMATE* Elevator Speech Template *floor by floor!*

- Each floor should convey *specific* information.
    o Start simply.
        - The first floor answers the question, Who?
            - It's your name.
    o Expand accordingly: When one-on-one and interest grows, and in front of a group as time permits.
        - Subsequent floors will offer more *specific* information about *What* you do.
            - I'll specify that information later.
            - Your message will have everyone *"sorting and sifting."*
                o Some will want more information and details.
                o Others will *Dis*-qualify themselves.

### Speech

An Elevator Speech that's delivered one-on-one or to a group is a mini-Presentation.

It is a *"Speaking* Opportunity!" and an important one because

*"Speaking Opportunities are Business, Career, and Leadership Opportunities!"*

That's my mantra! If you've heard me speak, read my books, or watched my videos, then you've heard it before. No one ever questions that statement. *Why would they?*

Since an Elevator Speech is a mini-Presentation, it should include all the elements of a meeting or seminar presentation. We'll look at those in a future chapter.

## *Multipurpose like a Swiss Army Knife!*

I wanted my Elevator Speech Template to be like my Swiss Army Knife–*Multipurpose.*

People deliver Elevator Speeches for
- *Themselves,* whether they are
  - Self-employed
  - Employed
  - Unemployed
- *Their workplace,* which could be a
  - Profit business
  - Nonprofit business
- *Other entities*
  - Clubs
  - Organizations
  - Associations

## *Flexible like a Yoga Expert*

For a variety of reasons, the *ULTIMATE* Elevator Speech Template had to be *flexible,* based on
- Audience size
- Type of audience
- Time constraints
- Parameters requested by the leader

## Not Only for Elevators!

We need a great Elevator Speech to deliver *whenever* and *wherever* called upon, including

- Elevators, of course!
- Escalators
- Stairs
- Moving sidewalks
- Bicycle rides
- Any assembly of people

## The Essence of a Great Elevator Speech

A great Elevator Speech should be

- Clear
- Concise
- Impactful

Here is the back-story and a great example of an inadvertent Elevator Speech that does those things extremely well.

I once owned a 1998 Ford Explorer. Even with more than 160,000 miles on it and a few dings and dents, I loved that car. (Minor body damage isn't all bad. People wave you through four-way stops and drivers give you greater leeway in parking lots!)

I needed brakes and was looking for a mechanic I could trust. I didn't want to pay for anything unneeded, and I sent out a request for recommendations to friends and family.

Danny's name came up several times. He worked at an independent garage that had a great reputation and he moonlighted on the side. I gave him a call. I told him what I had and what I was looking for. He said he could do the job. Then I started asking a bunch of questions about cars. Besides knowing how to drive, I know very little about vehicles and how they work. After he answered a few questions, he stopped me and gave one of the best Elevator Speeches I've ever heard. Here it is:

**"Fred, I went to Ranken Technical College.** (It's one of the top technical training schools in the country.)

**I'm ASE Certified.** (Like me, you've probably seen that blue and white logo in professional garages. It stands for **A**utomotive **S**ervice **E**xcellence.)

*You're in good hands!"*

"Done!" I said to myself. We hadn't discussed price. It didn't matter to me. With fourteen words in three sentences, Danny had established his credibility as an expert. I was *immediately* comfortable hiring him to work on my car.

I had one more question: "Danny, can we schedule the work for Saturday morning?"

He showed up at the scheduled time, did the job, and charged a fair price. Going forward, I called Danny whenever I needed a repair.

On several occasions, I accompanied Danny to an auto parts store to get a needed part. I didn't care if he picked out the most expensive or cheapest item because I trusted him. More than once, when I thought something was wrong with my car, like a shock absorber, he'd inspect it, tell me all was good, and send me on my way. He could have told me that all my shocks and struts needed replacement, and I wouldn't have questioned him. Of course, I gave him money for his time, but not nearly the amount he could have made making unnecessary repairs. He was a very honest person.

In fact, he was so honest that, after inspecting a transmission problem, he said, "Fred, this repair will cost you more than your car is worth. It's time you look for a replacement." Fortunately for me, the "Cash for Clunkers" program had recently been initiated by the government. Because of Danny's honesty, I jumped on the opportunity and got far more than the Explorer was worth. (*Thank you*, fellow taxpayers!)

That's a great story, isn't it! I love telling it and each time I do, audiences *GET IT! Your* Elevator Speech should have the same effect as Danny's Elevator Speech had on me.

Before we leave this chapter and look at my ULTIMATE Elevator Speech, I want to return to the story at the beginning of the chapter and tell you what Roy said that fired me up to build that template. The two-word phrase that grabbed everyone's attention was—*Hire me!*

Next, let's look at the *ULTIMATE* Elevator Speech Template to see how it was built and how *Hire me!* helps differentiate it from most Elevator Speeches.

# Chapter 4—My ULTIMATE Elevator Speech

What follows is *my* ULTIMATE Elevator Speech. It's the culmination of much research, testing, and tweaking. I deliver *this speech* whenever I'm offered a *Speaking* Opportunity in front of groups. The message moves "from the ground floor to the top floor." Since it covers everything that I want to tell an audience, I refer to it as "My ULTIMATE Elevator Speech."

When you read my ULTIMATE Elevator Speech in the section below, try to "hear" my voice, and start thinking about putting out the message into *your* world using *your* words.

Then read the speech a second time, perhaps aloud, because *that* activity is a great way to practice giving an Elevator Speech. Again, as you read the speech, start thinking about how each "floor" fits into *your* world.

Keep in mind that the following ULTIMATE Elevator Speech is *not* my Version 1.0. I've made *many* revisions, and you'll be doing the same.

My ULTIMATE Elevator Speech has eight floors. After going through the speech, we'll look closely at each floor to see how I crafted the message. My speech is approximately 37 seconds long.

## My ULTIMATE Elevator Speech

"Hello. My name is Fred Miller.

I'm a speaker, coach, and author.

The title of my *first* book is **NO SWEAT** *Public Speaking!*

Businesses, individuals, and organizations *hire me because* they want to improve their networking, public speaking, and presentation skills.

They do so because they know that *Speaking* Opportunities are *Business*, *Career*, and *Leadership* Opportunities.

They also know that we perceive really good speakers as *experts!* We like to work with *experts*. *Experts* can command more money for their products and services.

I show them how to develop, practice, and deliver *outstanding* presentations that engage, inform, and inspire audiences with– **NO SWEAT!"**

Note: I didn't proceed to the eighth floor. Sometimes I do, and I'll explain how to leverage this floor later.

*NO SWEAT Elevator Speech!*

# My ULTIMATE Elevator Speech— Floor by Floor

Now that you've read my speech, hopefully twice, what do you think?

My goal, which you will want to adopt for *your* Elevator Speech, is for my audience to know *exactly* what I do and my expertise for doing it. If you're one of my audience members, your next step is to *"sort and sift"* that information and decide if

- You want to have a conversation with me ASAP.
- You have no need for my services but will be comfortable contacting me in the future if something changes.
- Whether or not you'll ever need my services, you know what I do, your radar is up, and you'll refer me if you hear of anyone who needs what I offer.

If you liked my ULTIMATE Elevator Speech, keep reading, and I'll show you how I crafted it. If not, that's OK. My way is not the only way. Different speakers have different takes on Elevator Speeches. Check out several options, grab what works best for you, and do it your own way.

With that caveat in mind, come join me on the Elevator and tweak it to match *your* world.

*Fred E. Miller*

# Let's Get in the Elevator!

## *First Floor—Describe Who You Are*

*"Hello, my name is Fred Miller."*

That may be all someone wants to know about you—Your Name.

Often in one-on-one situations, people are just being polite, and learning your name is enough for them. If that's the case, it's OK.

If you find yourself in this situation during a "let's network before the event starts," move on to someone else. If you've done your homework before the event, you've targeted several people to meet. (More about this subject in a later chapter.) Seek them out and initiate your conversation like this:

"Bob, I'm Fred Miller. I saw your name on the attendee list and looked forward to meeting you."

Bob will probably respond, "Pleased to meet you, Fred. What do you do?"

*Great!* We're now on the Elevator, and I'm about to take Bob to the second floor.

## NO SWEAT Elevator Speech!

Note about Your Name: "Fred Miller" is a very simple name and easy to pronounce. Others, *not so much!*

**Example:**

I have a friend named Mike Ramatowski. My advice to him about introductions is to say, "Hi, my name is Mike." The challenge with a last name like Mike's is that listeners often get hung up on its spelling. "Is it s-k-y or s-k-i?" Then, down the rabbit hole they'll go. "What's the derivation?" "Where did your people come from?" If they know anyone else with the same last name, they may ask, "Are you related to...?" If that happens, your last name has become a distraction, and your listeners can miss the next floors of your Elevator Speech.

If your last name is difficult to pronounce or could raise questions like my friend Mike's, simply use your first name. If your Elevator Speech leads to making an appointment for a conversation, then you can share your last name along with the rest of your contact information.

If English is your second language, if you speak with a distinct accent, or if your first name is uncommon or difficult to pronounce, say your name twice s-l-o-w-l-y, and if helpful, relate it to something the listener will understand (e.g., a famous person or a word that rhymes with your name).

Another solution is to say your name without hurrying, spell it s-l-o-w-l-y, and say your name again.

## Second Floor—Describe What You Do

*"I'm a speaker, coach, and author."*

That's what I say. These words are clear, concise, and easily understood. People hearing them will usually perk up and, consciously or unconsciously, ask themselves:

- What does Fred speak about?
- What does Fred coach?
- What does Fred write about?

The next floors of my Elevator Speech will answer these questions.

In my ULTIMATE Elevator Speech workshops, I ask students to answer the question, "*What* do you do?" Many people respond with "I do a LOT of things!" Then, they proceed to name all those things. For some students, the list of services they offer and the items they sell gets long...very long. Occasionally, there's no common thread. Some of their lists are so long that no one will ever hire or refer them because listeners are confused and unable to recall everything.

I *GET IT!* I do a lot of things, too. But when it comes to Elevator Speeches, being **Concise** is one of the guidelines.

*Limit* the number of things you tell an audience you do to *no more than three.*

For several reasons, the number three is *magical!* (More on the *Magic of Three* in a future chapter.)

## NO SWEAT Elevator Speech!

- Three of your services and products probably compose 90 percent or more of your revenue.
- Generally, we can only remember three or four items without writing them down.
- Three offers *completeness*.
  - **One** for emphasis
    - Being a speaker gives you enormous credibility.
  - **Two** for comparison
    - Speaker—attendee
    - Author—reader
  - **Three** for completeness

We intuitively gravitate toward groupings of three. Now that you've been introduced to the *Magic of Three*, consider upping the number of services and products you mention in your Elevator Speech to three, even if you offer only one or two. Likewise, if you offer four or more services and products, drop that number to three for your Elevator Speech.

Another area of confusion arises when speakers aren't **Specific** enough when telling listeners what they do.

**Examples:**

- Systems analyst
  - Digestive system? HVAC system?
- Senior technical manager
  - I have no idea what that is.
- Training designer
  - Grade school training? Computer training? Dog training?

- IT professional
    - Hardware? Software?
- Engineer
    - Mechanical engineer? Electrical engineer? Choo-choo engineer?

In addition to being specific, your language should be **Simple**. People are rarely impressed with words they don't know. We feel stupid when we hear unfamiliar language. If you make me feel stupid, I won't hire or refer you.

**Examples:**

- I sell home and auto insurance.
    - Rather than "I sell insurance."
- I'm a Certified Public Accountant (CPA).
    - Rather than "I do accounting work."
    - While many people know that the letters "CPA" stand for Certified Public Accountant, other acronyms are less well known. Briefly explain or eliminate acronyms.
        - **Examples:**
            - EVP, Executive Vice President
            - CMO, Chief Marketing Officer
            - BSN, Bachelor of Science in Nursing
            - AS, Associate of Science
            - CTM, Competent Toastmaster
- I'm a criminal lawyer.
    - Rather than "I'm an attorney."
- I am a graphic designer.
    - Rather than "I'm a designer."
- I'm a pediatrician.
    - Rather than "I'm a physician."

If you're in a profession that may need explanation, offer clarification after stating *what* you do.

**Examples:**

- "I'm an ironmonger."
  "That's someone who sells things made of iron."
  "My specialty is yard sculpture."
- "I'm a pediatric hematologist/oncologist."
  "I treat children and teens with blood diseases and cancer."

You may think your profession doesn't need an explanation, but it just might. You'll never go wrong by clarifying.

**Example:**

Everyone doesn't know what a *sous chef* is. Explaining the profession by saying, "I'm the second in command in the kitchen and report to the head chef," clarifies *what* you do.

### Third Floor  Describe Your Expertise or Experience

"*The title of my first book is* **NO SWEAT Public Speaking!**"

When not pressed for time, I'll include the book's subtitle, "How to Develop, Practice, and Deliver *Outstanding* Presentations that Engage, Inform, and Inspire with–*NO SWEAT!*"

Society views people who have authored books as *experts*. That's one reason I've written several books and why I mention it on the third–or *Expertise*–floor.

**If you have never written a book, consider doing so for several reasons.**

- First, you will learn a *ton* of things you didn't know about your topic plus a bunch of other information, such as how to write a book, that will serve you well in the future.
    - That's my personal experience with writing books.
    - Noteworthy point: *This* book is the *second* edition because I learned so much *after* writing it the first time.
- Your book doesn't have to be lengthy.
    - There's nothing wrong with a short one.
- Online publishers like Amazon make it super easy to print books. Many such services are Print-on-Demand (POD).
    - In the past, authors were required to purchase a lot of books at one time to get their writing published. POD eliminated that expense and added flexibility as a benefit of being an author and publisher.
        - For example, check out Amazon's self-publishing arm, Kindle Direct Publishing; (KDP) likewise, LightningSource.com and Lulu.com are reputable self-publishing sites.
        - Additionally, you can hire a book consultant, often referred to as a Book Shepherd, to guide you from concept to completion and your first book signing event!
- I feel so strongly about the benefits of being an author–and the prestige and perception of expertise you'll receive–that I make this suggestion:

- If you haven't written a book, include the following sentence in your Expertise floor, "The title of my upcoming book is...."
    - You don't have say when it's going to be published, and you certainly can change the title.
    - Be aware that once you say you're writing a book, people will start asking,
        - "How's the book coming along?"
        - "When is your book going to be available?"
        - "When and where is your book signing going to be?"
        - All that pressure isn't all bad, will push you to complete a book, and will allow you to reap all the benefits I've derived by writing and publishing my own books.

## Other Areas of Expertise or Experience to Consider

- Number of years with a company or years of industry service
- Certifications
    - Be certain to explain them because many are industry specific.
- Awards
    - These can be from industries, municipalities, and associations and should also be explained.
- Patents, trademarks, and copywritten material, which are huge credibility builders
- Family owned!
    - What generation?
- Largest in your area

- One of a kind
- Educational degrees
    - Again, may need additional explanation
- Special skills
    - Example:
        - I know someone who is a Quicken expert, but also has a specific area of expertise using that software which few people have.
- Titles
    - Founder, CEO, president, owner, and general partner are important to state.
        - **Example:**
        I was once in the coffee service business. I had just landed a new piece of business, and the lady handling the paperwork asked my title. My company was very small. My partner was the CEO, and I was president. When I said I was the president of the company she *literally sat up straighter!* **Titles matter!**
    - Charge nurse
    - General manager
    - Supervisor
    - Team leader

You can include titles on the second floor of your Elevator Speech, too.

**Examples:**
- I'm the second-generation owner of City Hardware.
- I'm the vice president of sales for Southern Computer Services.
- I'm the fire chief for the City of _____ .

The third floor is powerful because it lends **Credibility** to your Elevator Speech and confirms *you* are an *expert* in the minds of your listeners!

Ask people who know you well to help you build this floor. Ask them to tell you what expertise and experience you have that others will find to be important. We're often too close to ourselves and *don't know what we know.*

## Fourth Floor WHY They Hire Me

> *"Businesses, individuals, and organizations hire me because they want to improve their networking, public speaking, and presentation skills."*

*"Hire me"* is the phrase my classmate, Roy Reichold, used in my sales class that everyone captured in their notes and subsequently incorporated into *their* Elevator Speeches. These two words motivated me to research Elevator Speeches, develop a signature presentation on the topic, and write the first edition of this book.

*"Hire me"* **is POWERFUL!**

*"Hire me"* grabs attention, *correct?* These words are powerful because they're not commonly used in an Elevator Speech. Most people say

- "I *work with* companies to...."
- "I *help* people to...."

The latter phrases are *wimpy!* They also fail to mention money. If you're independently wealthy and really *work with* and *help* for free–*good for you.* Continue using those phrases.

*"Hire me"* says:

- I'm proud of what I do.
- I'm *really* good at it.
- I *don't do this for free!*

*"Hire me"* can also be an excellent *Dis*-qualifier, especially when you're speaking one-to-one with someone. If the phrase turns them off–*good!* One goal of an Elevator Speech is to avoid wasting *major* time on *minor* possibilities. Everyone is *not* a prospect. You don't purchase everything you're offered. If your listeners' nonverbal communication (e.g., raised eyebrows or a shocked look on their faces) tells you *"Hire me"* hit a nerve, then it might be time to move on to someone else.

I've seen facial expressions like these and asked, "Are we finished, and should we move on and talk with others?" Usually, if listeners hesitate to answer this question, it's time to wish them well and leave. On the other hand, their replies have sometimes been, "*No!* I like that. Tell me more about *what* you do and how you do it."

During the Q&A segment of one of my Elevator Speech presentations, one attendee commented, "Seems to me, Fred, you have an *attitude* with that *"Hire me"* phrase.

My response was, "*You bet I do!* And it's a *good* attitude. Would you rather deal with people who are wishy-washy about their expertise, services, and products? *Not me!* I'm proud of what I do, and I'm very good at it. I'm not a fit for everyone and that's OK."

I understand that some people aren't comfortable using the phrase, "*Hire me.*" If you're one of those folks, *don't* use it. If that's how you feel, then the way you say it, your facial expressions, and your body language won't be in sync with the words. Nonverbal communication surpasses verbal communication when the two are in conflict, and your listeners will "see" the conflict.

A realtor in one of my classes used the following language: "People buying or selling homes *choose* me *because*...."I love it!

Other phrases that work equally well: Businesses, individuals, and organizations

- *Pay me* to....
- *Put me on their payroll* to....
- *Write me checks* to....
- *Give me money* to....
- *Invest in my expertise* to....
- *Spend money with me* to....

Depending on your profession, one of the following phrases could be a fit:

- Businesses, individuals, and organizations *become my clients*....
- People *become my patients*....
- Homeowners *have their major appliances serviced by us*....

An individual who is delivering an Elevator Speech for his or her company might say

- Businesses, individuals, and organizations *become our customers*....
- Associations *contract with our company*....
- Local, regional, and national governments *engage our services*....

Nonprofit organizations can use phrases like these: Businesses, individuals, and organizations

- Write us checks....
- Donate....
- Give us money....
- Volunteer....

The word **"*Because*"** is extremely important on this floor of your Elevator Speech. It's an "Influencer Word" that powerfully affects your listeners.

In his famous book, *Influence,* Dr. Robert Cialdini pointed out the word "*Because*" has a unique motivational effect.

Do you remember something like this from your childhood?

"Why do I have to do that, Mom?"

"Because I said so!"

Other examples:

"*Because* it's the right thing to do."

"*Because* we have to."

Use the word "*Because*" in your Elevator Speech *because* it makes a difference!

**NO SWEAT Elevator Speech!**

## *Fifth Floor Your WHY*

> *"They do so because they know that Speaking Opportunities are Business, Career, and Leadership Opportunities!"*

Sometimes I add, "That's my mantra! *No one ever challenges that statement. Why would they?"*

I *could,* but *wouldn't,* follow up this statement with the following:

"Are you *taking* and *making Speaking* Opportunities?" Such a question would continue the conversation.

However, this is an Elevator Speech, *not* a sales presentation. If this speech leads to a meeting and a conversation, I'll ask at that time. Remember that Elevator Speeches *sort and sift.* They are *not* for selling.

The fifth floor is *beyond* important. It's the **DNA of your Elevator Speech**. It's the center of *WHY* you do *what* you do and is derived from Simon Sinek's famous TED Talk, "How Great Leaders Inspire Action." In his talk, Sinek introduces the Golden Circle: Three concentric circles with

- *WHY* in the bullseye
- *HOW* in the middle ring
- *WHAT* in the outer ring

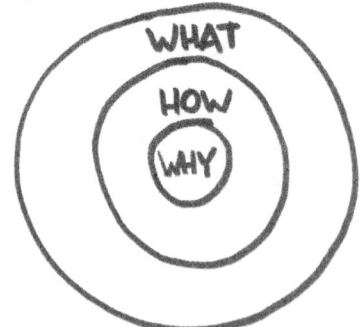

Sinek says you should "...*start with WHY* because it is central to **WHAT** you do." For more information, conduct a Google or Bing search using the following terms in quotation marks: "Simon Sinek, Start with WHY". Watching his videos and learning more about this concept are well worth your time.

I won't go through Sinek's presentation in detail, but his essential message and the core of your Elevator Speech is

**People don't buy WHAT you do; they buy *WHY* you do it.**

He explains that most companies start with WHAT.

**Example:**

"We're a big computer company. We make great computers with huge hard drives and lots of ram memory, and they are inexpensive. Want to buy one?"

(That's not a message that grabs anyone.)

A few firms like Apple *GET IT!* and start with *WHY.*

**Example:**

"Do you want to be creative?

Do you want to be more productive than you could ever imagine, and do you want to do it with equipment that's fun and easy to use?

We're Apple!"

(*YES!*)

My *WHY* for the fifth floor is *"They know that Speaking Opportunities are Business, Career, and Leadership Opportunities!"*

- If my listeners don't believe this statement, they don't need or want what I offer.
- That's OK! I'm not going to try to change their minds.
- The Goal, according to Simon Sinek, is not to do business with everyone who needs what you have.
- The Goal is to do business with *people who believe what you believe.*
- For you and me, *many* people resonate with our *WHY.*

Sinek also says,

- *WHY* is not profit. Profit is a result.
- He asks–and you need to answer these questions:
    o What is your purpose?
    o What is your cause?
    o What is your belief?
    o Why do you exist?
    o Why do you get up in the morning?

## *WHY* Examples:

"They *know* one of the best uses of their charitable contributions is *teaching* people to better their own lives."

"They *know* saving the lives of young children is a *far* better feeling than being super rich."

I urge you to watch Sinek's video several times and use his teachings to find *your WHY*. Once you do, *everything* changes!

### Sixth FloorMore WHY They Hire Me

> *"They also know that we perceive really good speakers as experts! We like to work with experts. Experts can command more money for their products and services."*

Those statements make sense, *don't they?*

**Other Sixth-Floor Examples:**

- They do so *because* they want it done *on* time, the *first* time, with *no* defects.
- They do so *because* the results of their volunteer work are *immediately* apparent, appreciated, and humbling.
- They do so *because* quality, safety, and dependability are their main concerns.
- They know an electrician with a lot of experience, knowledge, and certifications has seen and done it all!

Notice the "Magic of Three" that's being used!

Increase *your* credibility on the sixth floor *because* it matters!

*NO SWEAT Elevator Speech!*

## Seventh Floor─My Unique Selling Proposition (USP) What I Deliver

*"I show them how to develop, practice, and deliver outstanding presentations that engage, inform, and inspire with–NO SWEAT!"*

This sentence clearly states what someone who *hires* me can expect for me to deliver. It's sometimes referred to as a person's **Unique Selling Proposition (USP)**, and what the customer or client pays for.

What do *your* products and services do that makes *hiring you* a good decision? What problems do you solve? After spending money with you, what benefits will they realize?

The expression "***NO SWEAT***" is part of my personal and company branding. These are the last two words I use in my writing, podcasts, videos, and presentations. The phrase is short, easy to say, and memorable. In person or on video, I'll speak these two words while physically wiping my brow. If you have a brand, *this* is a great place to use it!

I use ***NO SWEAT*** to close all my Elevator Speeches. Here's why:

One of the most important **Rules of Public Speaking** has to do with the **Primacy/Recency Effect**. This effect is defined as the phenomenon in which audiences tend to best remember the *first* and *last* things they see and hear. That's why you want to use a strong opening and *stronger* closing whenever you're delivering presentations. The *last* thing your audiences see and hear is often the *first* thing they'll remember. Because an

Elevator Speech is a mini-Presentation, this rule applies. Long after an audience and I part company, they will remember—*NO SWEAT!*

If you don't have a strong personal brand and catch phrase, consider developing both.

**Seventh-Floor Examples:**

For a Business:
- "I file all tax-related transactions on time, with the correct taxing entity, and make certain all available discounts are taken."
- "We *guarantee* the job will be completed on time, within budget, without defects."

For a Nonprofit:
- "We make certain the skills and enthusiasm they bring as volunteers are maximized for themselves and the people they serve."
- "We put their contributions to work where the donor specifies and provide full transparency. That's why so many *regularly* write us checks."

## *Eighth Floor—Ask!*

The eighth floor is only used when delivering an Elevator Speech to one person. If a listener has joined you on the Elevator Ride thus far, he or she is probably interested in knowing more about *what* you do and how you work.

The next logical thing for you to ask is, "What do *you* do?"

While asking this question is certainly okay, asking it differently can help you to prospect.

## NO SWEAT Elevator Speech!

Consider taking the opportunity to ask a probing question and see if your audience of one is a prospect *or* knows someone who might need your products and services.

Asking the traditional question, "Do you know anyone who...?" requires only a 'yes' or 'no' answer. The response is usually, "No," and the conversation is over.

Try something different.

**Example:**
"You probably don't know any company or person who can benefit from networking, public speaking, and presentation skills training, *do you?*

Questioning in this manner will catch the listener off guard and usually spur thinking about someone (perhaps him- or herself) who might be a prospect.

**Other Examples of Eighth-Floor Questions:**

For a Business:
- "No one where you work has any challenges networking or giving presentations, *do they?*
- "Enough about me and what I do. How does your company handle networking and presentation skills training?"
- "Your tax filings are never late, *are they?*"
- "Your courier always delivers your packages on time, *don't they?*"
- "The cleaning service you use never misses anything, *do they?*"

For a Nonprofit:

- "How does your company decide where employees' volunteer efforts should be steered?"
- "What criteria do you use before making donations?"

# Chapter 5—Three Variations of Your Elevator Speech

The *ULTIMATE* Elevator Speech Template is a powerful *tool*. Much like a Swiss Army knife, the template was designed to be flexible and versatile.

## Skipping Floors

When delivering an Elevator Speech one-on-one or in groups, you will frequently be limited by time constraints.

However, once you've used the *ULTIMATE* Elevator Speech Template to develop your Elevator Speech floor-by-floor, you have the option of skipping floors. **Skips** can often be the answer to giving a great Elevator Speech when time is limited. (Elevators rarely stop on every floor.)

**Example:**
When your host gives you ten seconds (or fewer) to give an Elevator Speech

**First floor**

"I'm Fred Miller."

**Second floor**

"I'm a speaker, coach, and author."

## Fourth floor

"Businesses, individuals, and organizations *hire me because* they want to improve their **n**etworking, public speaking, and presentation skills."

You don't always have to start on the first floor. You can start on another floor and go down.

## Example:

Start on the Fifth Floor, your *WHY.*

### Fifth floor

As I raise my hand high, I'll ask, "Who believes *Speaking* Opportunities are *Business*,

*Career*, and *Leadership* Opportunities?" (Note: Raising *your* hand gets others to raise *their* hands, too.)

### First floor

"I'm Fred Miller."

### Second floor (modified)

"I speak, coach, and write about networking, public speaking, and presentation skills."

## The *EXPRESS* Elevator Speech

As previously mentioned, *Dis*-qualifying is a major goal of an Elevator Speech. This is especially true when you're speaking one-on-one because you don't want to waste *major* time on *minor* possibilities. This rule of thumb applies to you *and* the person with whom you're speaking.

## NO SWEAT Elevator Speech!

As people are listening to your Elevator Speech, they're *sorting and sifting* the information you present to determine the next step they might take regarding your products and services. Again, *Dis*-qualifying themselves is one possibility. Your goal is to let them know *exactly* what you offer and provide them the necessary information to refer you if you're not a good fit for them.

The EXPRESS Elevator Speech articulates what you do...
- Clearly
- Concisely
- Impactfully

Here's how the *EXPRESS* Elevator Speech works.

When someone asks the question, "What do you do?"–or it's your turn to answer the question in a group situation–here's the formula:

1. Answer the question by *ask*ing a question.
2. Tell the audience what you deliver: Your Unique Selling Proposition (USP). (7$^{th}$ Floor).
3. State your WHY. (5$^{th}$ Floor).
4. Ask another question.

**Example:**

"Fred, what do you do?"

1. "Thanks for asking. I'm going to *answer* that question by *asking* a question. Have you ever been to an event, watching and listening to a speaker, and thought to yourself,

    "'*Wow!* That guy is great! He's articulate, authentic, and very entertaining. Obviously, he has a passion for what he's doing, and I'm getting a *lot* from this presentation. *Man*, I wish *I* could do that.'"

P-a-u-s-e

2. *"I'm the guy people hire* to develop, practice, and deliver *outstanding* presentations like *that!"*
3. At this point, if I'm speaking one-on-one, I'd like that person to say, *"Really!* I need to find out how you do that." We would then exchange contact information and agree to have a follow-up conversation.
4. If I received no response or was speaking in front of a group, I'd go to Step 2 and state my *WHY.*
5. "Everyone who *hires me* knows, *Speaking* Opportunities are *Business, Career,* and *Leadership* Opportunities."
6. Next, I'd ask another question.
7. "You probably don't know anyone who wants to improve their public speaking and presentation skills, *do you?"*

    Possible responses:
    a. A definite "NO, I don't need that!"
        - I've *Dis*-qualified them.
            - *Good!* No need to waste my time.
    b. A question that signals they *are* a prospect
        - **Example:** "How does that work?"
            - *Great!* We'll exchange contact information and agree to have a conversation in the future.
    c. A referral
        - **Example:** "I have a friend who has an important presentation coming up and might need some coaching."

- *Super!* I'll gather as much information as possible and follow-up by contacting them.

If I'm speaking in front of a group, the question is rhetorical. Again, the audience will be *sorting and sifting* information to determine if they are (or aren't) a good fit and if there's a next step. Hopefully, they'll also be thinking of someone who would benefit from my offerings.

## The Twitter-Type Elevator Speech

Sometimes, when you're speaking in front of a large group or operating under time constraints, the leader may say, "Please deliver your Elevator Speech in *twenty words or less."*

This situation can be challenging but well worth the effort. With a bit of tweaking, some of the floors in your ULTIMATE Elevator Speech can stand on their own for a **Twitter-Type Elevator Speech**.

As with most editing activities, less is more. People want us to get to the point and answer the question, "What's the bottom line?" (Twitter has dramatically increased the speed of the communication world.)

One big downside of Twitter is the growing use of abbreviations. Their use affects conventional communication especially when we're trying to be articulate, but also required to communicate effectively in Tweeting mode.

Here are a few of my Twitter-Type Elevator Speeches:

**Second floor (modified)**—*What* I do

"I speak, coach, and write about networking, public speaking, and presentation skills."

- 12 words
- 85 characters with spaces

**Fourth floor**—What I deliver and why clients hire me

"Businesses, individuals, and organizations *hire me because* they want to improve their networking, public speaking, and presentation skills."

- 18 words
- 139 characters with space

**Seventh floor**—What I offer my clients, or my Unique Selling Proposition (USP)

"I'm *hired* to show people how to develop, practice, and deliver outstanding presentations that engage, inform, and inspire with—*NO SWEAT!*"

- 21 words
- 137 characters with spaces

# Chapter 6—The Elevator Speech: Delivering It

Before discussing Delivering your Elevator Speech, let's start by acknowledging the following important fact:

The goal of all communication — verbal, written, or visual — is the same. You want your audience, be it one or thousands, to *GET IT!* as quickly as possible!

They may not agree with everything you say.

They may not agree with *anything* you say.

However, if they don't *GET IT!* there can be no meaningful conversation going forward.

You can have a superior Elevator Speech or presentation, but if you don't deliver it well, the audience will not *GET IT!*

An effective Elevator Speech or presentation consists of
- The words you choose
- How you say them
- How your nonverbal communication reinforces them

Every presentation, including your Elevator Speech, has two Components:

1. Content
    - The message you want the audience to GET!

- In your Elevator Speech, that's the information on each floor

2. Delivery
    - *How* you present the message
    - Each floor of your Elevator Speech has details to deliver about you

The **Delivery** Component of a presentation has two Parts:

1. Verbal
    - The **words** you use to inform, inspire, tell your stories, and more
2. Nonverbal
    - **Vocal cues**: All the oral aspects of sound except for words, including silence
    - **Body movements**: Voluntary and involuntary

For the **Verbal** part of Your Delivery, your **words** should be simple and easily understood. You won't impress your audience with words they don't know. You'll make them feel stupid and lose them.

Also avoid buzz words, acronyms, industry jargon, regional lingo, and slang words. Even if you think your audience will understand those terms, they may not. You probably don't have any idea how long your audience has been in your industry, and the industry they come from (or the region where they live) could have different interpretations of your words.

*In all presentations, Nonverbal Communication surpasses Verbal Communication when it comes to assigning meaning.*

## NO SWEAT Elevator Speech!

*We believe what we see.*

One famous example was the first televised Presidential debate between Richard Nixon and John F. Kennedy on September 25, 1960. (Search YouTube for this debate, and you'll "see" what I mean.)

Television displays were only black and white at the time. Richard Nixon was a man who had a "five o'clock shadow" in the morning and didn't want to use makeup to cover it. His upper lip was wet with sweat, he didn't always look directly into the camera, and he appeared "shifty-eyed" to many. He had recently been in the hospital and lost weight, and his suit was ill-fitting. To many he appeared nervous and untrustworthy.

Kennedy looked healthy and youthful, appeared calm and confident, understood the power of television, and spoke directly to the camera and people who were watching.

Interestingly enough (and important to someone delivering an Elevator Speech or formal presentation), the audience that heard the debate on the radio thought Nixon won. Those watching on television believed Nixon looked nervous and dishonest and, therefore, thought Kennedy won. Kennedy won the election.

### Note it Remember it Practice it!
### (The *Magic of Three!*)

Because Nonverbal Communication surpasses Verbal Communication when the two messages are different (or competing), that's where we'll start our discussion about delivering your Elevator Speech.

## Nonverbal Communication: Vocal Cues

Let's begin by saying **You Want to Avoid Being Mechanical in Your Delivery.**

We've all heard people deliver an Elevator Speech as if it was a pre-recorded message. It's almost as if the speaker pressed a switch to start playing an audio file.

Often, the message is delivered too quickly to be understood and in a monotonous, boring manner. If you could locate an on/off switch on such a speaker, you'd be searching for it, and others would cheer when you turned it off.

When delivering your Elevator Speech, it's OK to *struggle* a bit. Doing so will make you seem *real*. Smooth and slick rarely translates to authenticity.

Here are some important **Vocal Cues** that make a difference when you're delivering an Elevator Speech.

## Enunciation and Pronunciation

**Enunciation** is the extent to which you articulate your words clearly and distinctly.

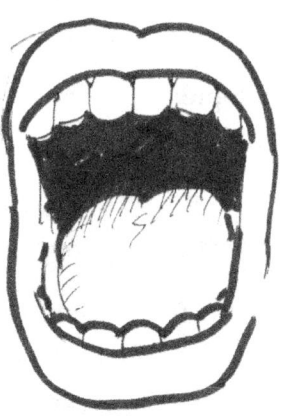

**Pronunciation** is the way you say your words, based on your upbringing and the region where you live. Spelling doesn't determine Pronunciation and is one reason that English can be challenging for people who speak English as a second language.

- If people cannot decipher the words that you're speaking, they'll never GET IT!
- Speak clearly and distinctly so that your words can be understood.
    - Avoid mumbling or slurring words.
- People with strong regional or foreign accents often need to work on Pronunciation.
    - For example, the stereotypical Southern drawl, old school New Jersey accent, and East Indian Hindi accent can be difficult to understand if they are particularly "thick" or pronounced.

## Inflection

**Inflection,** or **Emphasis**, is the weight or stress you place on a word to underscore its importance in a sentence. Changing the words that you emphasize can dramatically change your entire meaning.

**Pitch** and **Intonation** are components of Inflection. Pitch refers to the highness and lowness of your voice. Intonation is the rise and fall of your voice in spoken language.

**Example:**
"I did not borrow his car."

Consider how changing the Emphasis on *a single* word in the sentence can change the entire meaning!

- *I* did not borrow her car.
    - o  Perhaps her brother did.
- I did not *borrow* her car.
    - o  Sorry. I took it for a joy ride and should have asked permission first.
- I did not borrow *her* car.
    - o  I borrowed her sister's car.
- I did not borrow her *car*.
    - o  I borrowed her motorcycle.

The opposite of Emphasis is speaking in a **Monotone**. Don't be like a robot or the R2-D2 character in Star Wars and speak in a monotone because doing so can be boring and hard to understand.

## Speech Rate

**Speech Rate** is how fast or slowly you are speaking. Think of a metronome on top of a piano.

## NO SWEAT Elevator Speech!

In my experience listening to countless Elevator Speeches, many people deliver them too fast, some *way* too fast, and almost indiscernibly. This happens for several reasons.

- Fear of Public Speaking, which is shared by many people. In later chapters, we'll discuss this fear and ways to reduce it.
- The speaker doesn't realize how much time is allotted for his or her Elevator Speech and zips through it in order to sit down and listen to the next one.
    o Often, the designated time is 30 seconds, and the speaker finishes in 15 seconds.
    o The result is that the audience can't make sense of what they've heard and has no idea what the speaker does.

The opposite of speaking too fast is speaking too slowly. Slow rates of speech can be interpreted negatively and lose an audience.

**Varying your Speech Rate will keep the audience's attention**. It's the best way to deliver an Elevator Speech and increases the odds your audience will *GET IT!*

**The key is to practice and time yourself.** Thirty seconds last longer than most people think. Use a stopwatch and check yourself using the *ULTIMATE* Elevator Speech Template. Start with three floors and add others. *My* Ultimate Elevator Speech is only 37 seconds long.

## Pausing

**Pausing** is being silent. It's tough for most of us to do because the absence of sound can be unsettling. This is especially true if we're supposed to be speaking and telling people *who* we are and *what* we do. We're anxious to fill the silence with our voices.

The famous French composer Claude Debussy said, "Music is the silence between the notes."

Pausing is an exceptionally important vocal cue because

- It gives an audience (of one to many) time to absorb and process what you say.
    - The extra time helps them to understand your message.
- If you use humor and people are laughing, *not* pausing will cause them to miss something.
    - Don't talk over laughter.
- Pausing is an opportunity to emphasize something important that you want the audience to know.
    - **Example:**
    "Think about this statement. **(P-A-U-S-E)** *Speaking* Opportunities are *Business, Career,* and *Leadership* opportunities!" **(P-A-U-S-E)** People who *take* and *make* those *Speaking* Opportunities **(P-A-U-S-E)** *grow* their businesses, *advance* their careers, and *increase* their leadership roles."

## Volume

**Volume** is the loudness or softness of your voice.

Shouting will get your audience to pay attention, but when done to the extreme will irritate them. Most of us don't like to be shouted at. Shouting can also hurt your vocal cords.

Speaking softly, but not too softly so they can hear you, also garners your audience's attention because when we tell secrets we often whisper.

## Quality

**Quality** refers to the unique resonance of your voice. It may be husky, hoarse, or harsh sounding, or carry a nasal tone.

For example, consider the unique voices of James Earl Jones, Morgan Freeman, Sam Elliott, and Howard Cosell.

**Vocal Fry** is an annoying voice quality. Think the Valley Girl-sounding voices of Kim Kardashian and Katy Perry. Vocal Fry is defined as the lowest register (tone) of your voice that's characterized by a deep, raspy, creaky sound. Avoid allowing your voice to sound raspy or creaky because your audience may make negative assumptions about your intelligence, competence, and attractiveness.

## Nonword Sounds

Some **Nonword Sounds** can also be used for effect when speaking.

Examples include "Huh," "mmh," and "aah." These sounds, especially when combined with great facial expressions, can convey powerful messages to your audience.

## Forms of Nonverbal Communication

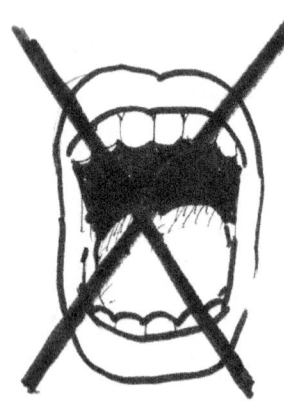

**Nonverbal Communication** (including Vocal Cues) falls into two categories:

1. **Voluntary,** or conscious behaviors
2. **Involuntary,** or unconscious behaviors

The audience doesn't care if your Nonverbal Communication is Voluntary or Involuntary. *They believe what they see.* If there's a conflict between what they hear (i.e., your words) and what they see, Nonverbal Communication will triumph. If you roll your eyes when you hear something you disagree with, or if you seem aloof or disengaged when someone else is speaking, be keenly aware *that*'s the message your audience will receive.

An example of *total* Nonverbal Communication is a professional mime. Have you ever seen one perform? I saw a performance in San Francisco, and it was *amazing!* With no words, the performer's message was exceptionally clear. That's the power of Nonverbal Communication.

Note: Nonverbal Communication is a two-way street.

**NO SWEAT Elevator Speech!**

As you're delivering your Elevator Speech, recipients are responding with *their* Nonverbal Communication.

## Eye Contact

"The eyes are the gateway to the soul."

"I can see it in his eyes!"

We've all heard these and similar phrases. They mean our eyes are an exceptionally expressive part of our face, and others can derive much about us by looking at them.

- Eyes can twinkle, smile, and pierce.
- Eyes can express
    - Surprise
    - Shock
    - Disbelief
    - Sympathy
- Eyes can say we're
    - Sleepy
    - Inattentive
    - Thoughtful

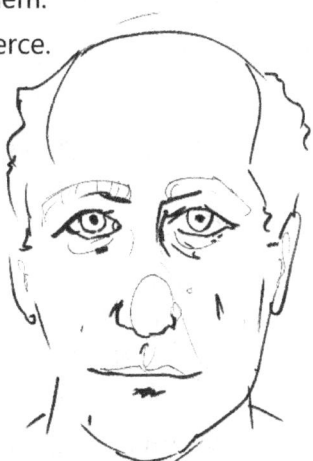

Whether you're speaking to another person or a group, make eye contact because doing so...

- Conveys honesty and integrity
    - *Not* looking someone in the eye makes them wary of your honesty.
    - Notable cultural exceptions: Native American and most Latin-American, Asian, and African societies
- Shows confidence in your competence

When you're in front of an audience, visually survey the group until you see someone who is GETTING your message. Look him or her directly in the eye, finish your thought, and move on to another attentive person in a different part of the room. Continue this course of action until you've finished your Elevator Speech.

Don't be a "searchlight beacon" that moves your head mechanically from side to side scanning the audience. Doing so will make you appear artificial.

*Don't* stare! No one likes to be stared at because it makes us feel uncomfortable.

## Facial Expressions

### *Smile!*

- A smile is *universally* understood and warms people up.
- Smiling is contagious.
    - I refer to a smile as a Non-Physical Hug.
    - When you give one, you get one right back!
- Warm up your audience of one or hundreds by offering a big smile before delivering your Elevator Speech!

## Universal Facial Expressions include
- Fear
- Anger
- Surprise
- Disgust
- Happiness
- Sadness
- Contempt

# Gestures

I'm sure you've seen people who *talk with their hands.* Many of us do. It's especially noticeable when they feel strongly about what they're saying.

As mentioned earlier, almost all forms of Nonverbal Communication can be voluntary or involuntary.

Gestures allow us to express a variety of thoughts and feelings.

**Examples:**
- Throwing our hands in the air—*I give up!*
- Moving a hand forcefully up and down–*Making a point*
- Snapping our fingers—*I just remembered!*
- Holding our head in our hands—*Worry*
- Slapping our forehead—*I should have known that answer*
- Tapping on our chest or head—*In my heart* or *on my mind*
- Shrugging our shoulders—*I don't know* or *who cares?*
- Cocking our head in a specific direction—*Over there* or *let's go*
- Pounding a fist into the palm of our hands—*I'm mad!*

- Holding our stomach—*I'm not feeling well*
- Rubbing our tummy—*Tastes good!*

Gestures aren't limited to what we do with our fingers, hands, and arms. They also include

- Legs–kicking our feet—I'm going to kick you out of class!
- Knees–alternately lifting our legs parallel to the ground with knees bent, as in marching
- Feet–raising and lowering our bodies on our toes

When delivering my Elevator Speech or giving workshops to groups, I'll often start with one hand, palm down to my side, indicating I'm talking about the First Floor of an Elevator Speech. I'll "deliver" that floor then go on to "deliver" successive floors, raising my hand in incremental amounts for each floor.

## *Gesture Guidelines*

- Exaggerate them when you're in front of a large audience.
- Be certain they're in sync with your verbal message.
  - If not, your gestures will override your words and may fail to convey the message you want to send.

Important Note about Gestures:

*They are not all universal.*

Different cultures use and interpret gestures in different ways. A seemingly innocuous gesture in one country or culture could be an obscene, even insulting gesture in another country or culture.

**Example:**

In the United States, a *thumbs up* gesture means *great going!*

In other countries, the same gesture has an entirely *not nice* meaning.

With many countries growing more and more culturally diverse, it's important to be aware of this fact. Being insensitive to different interpretations of gestures can negate an otherwise good presentation.

## Body Language

In addition to gestures, we convey a variety of messages with our bodies.

## Posture

- Stand straight with shoulders back and chest out, as a military guard does.
    - This stance displays *confidence in your competence.*
- *No* slouching, leaning, or fidgeting with your hands
    - These behaviors display nervousness and lack of conviction.
- No stuffing your hands into your pockets
    - I usually empty my pockets before formal presentations.
    - I recall being in the military where some had their pockets sewn shut!
- *No* standing in a "fig-leaf" position (hands on top of each other below your beltline)
    - This position may seem natural but distracts from your message.
    - Some think this stance sends a message that the speaker is trying to protect him- or herself.

- *No* folding your arms across your chest
  - Many interpret this stance as being defensive or holding something back.
- *No* assuming "parade rest," a military position with hands crossed behind your back
- *No* Superman or Wonder Woman poses (i.e., placing your fists on your hips)
  - These positions can send the wrong message (e.g., anger, frustration)
- Posture also applies to sitting before and after you speak.
  - Have the mindset that you are always on stage.
  - Sit upright and look at the person who is speaking.
  - If you're slouching, checking email, or yawning while you're waiting for your turn to give your Elevator Speech, you're not sending the optimal message to others.
  - The same applies *after* you deliver your Elevator Speech.

## Body Movement

When delivering your Elevator Speech (or any presentation), keep your body movements to a minimum. If you have a specific reason to move, do so *intentionally*. *Not* doing so will distract from your message.

**Examples:**
With a large audience, you might walk purposely to one side of the stage, addressing those seated in front of you, then walk intently and confidently to the other side of the stage and do the same.

Be equally deliberate with your gestures — for example, when you raise your hand high and turn your body so the audience will *see* your gesture.

*Don't...*

- Sway back and forth
    - **Example:** I once evaluated a fellow Toastmaster who swayed back and forth throughout his presentation. One of my critique questions–as *I* swayed back and forth–was, "Michael, did you ever spend time at sea?"
- Move up and down on your toes
- Balance on one foot
- Cross your legs while standing
- Do knee bends
- Stretch shoulders, back, or hips

Note: TED Talks are presented while standing in a trademark red circle that restricts any movement outside the circle to avoid distracting the audience.

## Clothing

What you wear should be suitable and proper for the subject, audience, and occasion–and should never be distracting. Likewise, avoid ostentatious clothing and fancy jewelry.

### *Examples where you can "see" my point:*

I once mentioned this advice during a presentation, and a lady in the audience agreed. She said, "I know exactly what you mean. I asked a co-worker who had just returned from a presentation, "How was the speaker?" Her reply was, *"She had this beautiful scarf draped across her body."*

One of the things people remember most from President Obama's first inauguration is Aretha Franklin's ruby red embroidered hat. The hat received so much attention that she donated it to the Smithsonian Museum. Eventually, this stunning piece of memorabilia wound up in Barak Obama's Presidential Library.

*Good* examples–because they *don't* distract audiences–include

> Steve Job's black turtleneck sweaters
>
> Rachel Maddow's black business suits
>
> Anderson Cooper's white shirts and thin, dark ties
>
> Johnny Cash's all black attire
>
> Mark Zuckerberg's non-descript hoodies

## A Final Note about *In*voluntary Nonverbal Communication

As noted earlier, we sometimes send nonverbal messages *in*voluntarily. The results may not be in sync with our intentions as speakers because

*People believe what they see.* An audience may "see" us as disinterested, bored, or "speaking out of both sides of our mouth" and worse.

**Example:**
If I said, "I'm really enjoying this event and meeting people like

you," then yawn and look at my watch, what message do you receive?

**Examples of *In*voluntary Nonverbal Communication...when you're not being mindful:**

- Facial expressions
    - Yawning
    - Laughing
    - Frowning
    - Raising eyebrows
    - Wincing
- Gestures
    - Fidgeting
    - Scratching
    - Tapping fingers
- Body language
    - Slouching
    - Leaning
    - Toe tapping
- Body movement
    - Random pacing
- Clothing
    - Loud fabric patterns
    - Flashy watches and jewelry
    - Stained attire
    - Wrinkled clothes
    - Missing buttons
    - Ill-fitting garments

It's imperative to be aware of the messages that your Nonverbal Communication conveys. *All* components, parts, and elements of a presentation must be in sync. Being mindful that the wrong

*Fred E. Miller*

Nonverbal Communication can torpedo your Elevator Speeches will make you a better communicator!

Do you **"See"** what I mean?

# Chapter 7—Bonus Tips for a Great Elevator Speech

### Greet People!

Before the 2020 pandemic, we shook hands when greeting new folks or long-time friends. "Smile. Look them directly in the eye, give them a firm handshake, and hold that hand a bit longer than normal," was my suggestion.

I prided myself on the Meet-and-Greet element of networking and making the rounds before everyone was asked, "Please stand. Tell us *who* you are and *what* you do. Give us your Elevator Speech!"

As of this writing, we bump fists, elbows, or the air when greeting others. We still look into each other's eyes and notice each other's facial expressions. Doing so is still an important activity.

## Continually Take the Temperature of Your Audience

In discussing the delivery of your Elevator Speech in earlier chapters, I mentioned that Nonverbal Communication is a two-way street between you and your audience (of one or many). They are consciously or unconsciously "reading" you. *You* should be doing the same.

Look for eye contact, facial expressions, and body language to determine if they are *GETTING IT!* If the message you are conveying results in looks of confusion, disbelief, or lack of interest, you'll need to review and possibly rework your Elevator Speech and your delivery.

## Interact with Your Audience

Interaction engages people and increases the odds they'll *GET IT!*

Ways to Interact

- Ask questions
  - When you ask a question, the audience will feel compelled to craft an answer and get ready to respond. Preparing answers to your questions requires more of their attention than just absorbing your message.
  - **Example from my Elevator Speech:**
    "We perceive really good speakers as *Experts*. We like to work with *Experts, don't we?"* (I pause to let the question sink in.

- o The question *"Don't we?"* requires a verbal "Yes!" or an affirmative head nod.
- Request physical actions
  - o Asking your audience to move their hands, arms, or legs is another tactic for engaging them.
  - o **Example from one of my presentations about Elevator Speeches:**
    "Raise your hand high if you've changed, tweaked, or trashed your Elevator Speech in the last year!" (By raising *my* hand high as I start that sentence, more audience hands go up than if I had not opened with that gesture.)

## Buzz Words

Every single industry, culture, and region has buzz words, acronyms, and techno-speak that are specific to its members. Too often, people in these groups think the universe understands them. They *do not. Avoid using buzz words!*

We rarely impress people by using words and phrases they don't know. Doing so makes them feel ignorant or stupid, and that feeling will cause them to quickly lose attention and torpedo any chance of future business or referrals.

*We see the emperor without clothing, but no one says anything!*

**Example:**
One of the groups I work with is financial advisors. They talk to

audiences about exchange traded funds (ETFs), mutual funds, and derivatives. Their prospects usually nod their heads up and down as if they understand those terms. *Most don't* and won't become clients.

**Use simple language** in your Elevator Speech if you want them to *GET IT!*

# Filler Words

Toastmasters is a nonprofit educational organization that operates clubs worldwide to promote communication, public speaking, and leadership. I was a member for many years and highly recommend joining to anyone who wants to improve his or her speaking and leadership skills.

Each Toastmasters meeting has several roles that participants can play, including Toastmaster of the Evening, Grammarian, Speaker, and others.

One role of note is the 'Ah Counter.' The Ah Counter's job is to listen to speakers and note whenever they are using the word "Ah" or other filler words. **Filler Words** are words (and phrases) that speakers use to fill silence while they're speaking. They add no value to the message. Instead they keep the speaker going until he or she completes a sentence.

**Examples:**
- Like
- You know
- Um
- Err

- OK?
- So
- Ah

Filler Words distract from a speaker's message. Some Toastmasters clubs ask their Ah Counters to ding a bell or click a clicker to alert a speaker whenever he or she uses a filler. Until many of the speakers hear that 'ding' or 'click,' they aren't conscious of the fact that they even use Filler Words in their speeches.

Awareness is the first step in eliminating Filler Words. That's why practicing your Elevator Speech, recording your practice sessions, and listening to your recordings are important. Rather than filling silence, *embrace* the silence and p-a-u-s-e. Pausing is *powerful.*

## Cliché

Have you ever heard anyone say...?
- "In his (or her) wheelhouse"
- "Think outside the box"
- "Give 110%"
- "Getting ahead of his skis!"
- "Sucking all the oxygen out of the room"

*Many, many* times is probably your answer. Perhaps, *too many* times! These are clichés.

**Clichés** are words and phrases that were novel and interesting at one time. However, they've been used so many times that they've lost their original effect. Many are too general and not specific to the speaker's Elevator Speech. Clichés are uninspiring and should be left out of your Elevator Speech.

Using Clichés is as bad as retelling old jokes or recounting Abe Lincoln or George Washington stories about honesty. *We've heard them multiple times!*

WHY to Avoid Using Clichés

- They make you seem boring, and who wants that label? When you use a Cliché, you're telling your audience you lack originality, and they may stop listening because they think you're rehashing information they already know.
- You lose credibility. Your audience won't see you as an *expert* if you can't come up with a better description than a Cliché. They've already heard them too many times.
- Clichés are imprecise. *Specific* details and explanations make better evidence than generalizations and overly used phrases.

How to Rid Your Elevator Speech of Clichés

- First, be aware you are using them. Making an audio recording of your Elevator Speech and listening with a critical ear are goods way to catch them.
- Say *precisely* what you want to say. Keeping your message simple usually works best, and *less* is *more*.

**Bottom Line:** *Avoid Clichés like the plague!* (Oops! That's definitely a Cliché!)

*NO SWEAT Elevator Speech!*

## Taglines

**Taglines** are unique slogans or catchphrases that tell people *who* you are and *what* you stand for. They can be part of your brand and differentiate *your* Elevator Speech from the ones that most people deliver. People remember great Taglines and associate them with you, your products, and your services.

Consider the following Taglines:
- "If it's Sunday, it's *Meet the Press.*" (Meet the Press, the U.S. television news program)
- "You're in good hands with Allstate." (Allstate Insurance)
- "Just do it!" (Nike)
- "The quicker picker upper" (Bounty Paper Towels)
- "Think Different" (Apple Computers)

**Example:**
I end all my Elevator Speeches and presentations with the following Tagline:

> *"... absolutely, positively. There's no doubt in my mind. Your Elevator Speech (Presentation) will be–NO SWEAT!"*

If I'm speaking to folks who have heard my presentations before, many will wipe their brow as I do when closing my presentation and saying the words–*NO SWEAT!*

How cool is that!

## Be Conversational

An excellent Elevator Speech, like a great presentation, is delivered in a conversational manner. You're not lecturing the audience.

Like most conversations, an Elevator Speech should
- Offer a varying pace of delivery
- Use simple language
- Exclude profanity or inappropriate language
- Consist of meaningful pauses
- Emphasize certain words and phrases
- Include eye contact, facial expressions, and gestures
- Contain no filler words and phrases that distract from your message

## Quotable Quotes

How cool would it be to have people quote you from your Elevator Speech?

**Quotable Quotes** are similar to Taglines and, in fact, you can make one your own. They're something you say that is substantive, memorable, and easy for others to repeat. Quotable Quotes must be relevant to the content of your message and something you want others to embrace and believe. Ideally, they should be no longer than one sentence.

**Examples of Quotable Quotes and Their Authors:**
- *"Love the life you live, live the life you love."*– Bob Marley
- *"Never, never, never give up."*–Winston Churchill
- *"Failure is the opportunity to begin again, more intelligently."*–Henry Ford

### NO SWEAT Elevator Speech!

- *"We may have all come on different ships, but we're in the same boat now."* –Martin Luther King

*My* Quotable Quote in my Elevator Speech is:

*"Speaking* Opportunities are *Business, Career,* and *Leadership* Opportunities!"

To add impact, I'll add "That's my mantra." No one ever challenges that statement. Why would they!

Think about your offerings and what you want your audience to take away from your Elevator Speech. Experiment with different Quotable Quotes. Eventually, you'll come up with something that others will be repeating and attributing to you!

## The Rule of Three

Throughout history, the number **THREE** has been used in a variety of compelling ways.

**Examples:**
- Three blind mice
- Three strikes–you're out!
- Ready–Aim–Fire!
- The third time's the charm.
- The Father, the Son, and the Holy Ghost
- I came. I saw. I conquered.

- Good–Better–Best
- Low–Medium–High
- A Three-Act play is the standard structure in Hollywood.
- In a speech, we present an Opening–Body–Conclusion.
- When telling jokes, the formula is Setup–Anticipation–Punch Line.

THREE is also a *magical* number when it comes to great Elevator Speeches.

Here's why:

We want the audience to remember our message. Most people can recall no more than three or four items at a time. Using THREE items, adjectives, or descriptions will increase the odds that your audience *GETS IT!* and remembers your message.

In his book, *Writing Tools: 50 Essential Strategies for Every Writer,* Roy Peter Clark provides insights about the magic of the number three. He suggests the following:
- Use **one** for emphasis
    - **Zoom** is a great way to hold meetings virtually.
- Use **two** for comparison
    - Fast–slow
    - Up–down
    - Black–white
- Use **three** for completeness
    - See examples below

- Use **four or more** for a list
    o A shopping or to-do list

**Examples of the Magic of Three:**
- *Speaking* Opportunities are *Business*, *Career*, and *Leadership* Opportunities!
- I *Speak*, *Coach*, and *Write* about *Networking, Public Speaking*, and *Presentation Skills*.
- Avoid using *Buzz Words, Acronyms*, or *Techno-Speak*.

Here is the Rule of Three Using Alliteration: **Alliteration** is the occurrence of the same letter or sound at the beginning of words that are adjacent or closely connected.
- If we want the audience to GET IT! we need to Educate, Entertain, and Explain.
- A great Elevator Speech is Clear, Concise, and Consistent.

**Fact:**

We create a lot of such groupings intuitively.

Now that you know the power of THREE, do *this:*
- When you're using TWO items, adjectives, or descriptions—add one more.
- If you're presenting FOUR OR MORE of something, drop *down* to THREE.

That's the Importance of the Magic of Three!

Use Groupings of Three for Elevator Speeches, Presentations, and General Communication

Understand it–Practice it–Use it!

*Fred E. Miller*

# Props

Your audience has three **Learning Styles**.

- Visual
    - 65% of us learn by *seeing* (or sight).
        - That's why images and videos are effective ways to help people *GET IT!*
        - People will say, "I *see* what you mean."
- Auditory
    - 35% of us learn by *listening*.
        - The popularity of audio books and podcasts confirms this learning style.
        - Folks will say, "I *hear* what you're saying."
- Kinesthetic
    - 5% of us learn by *doing*.
        - We prefer to learn by doing something ourselves rather than listening to a lecture or watching a demonstration.
        - I have a friend who regularly fills notebooks when attending seminars.

Appealing to two or more of these learning styles increases the odds that people will *GET IT!*

**Props** are physical objects that appeal to visual learners. *Showing* what you're talking about can quickly and dramatically convey your message.

**Examples:**
- A doctor who holds a stethoscope in the air
- A glassblower who displays one of his or her beautiful creations

- A financial planner who clasps a wad of cash for people to see

Caveats for Using Props
- Make sure they are relevant to what you do in your profession.
- Use them to make your point, then immediately put them away. Otherwise, they can distract from your message.
- If necessary, provide an explanation (e.g., "A stethoscope is one of my most prized diagnostic tools.").

In the absence of a physical Prop (or photograph or diagram), *verbally* make the audience *see* what you're saying.

**Example:**

*"Picture this.* There was a bad ice storm last night and many power lines are down. A utility truck with a bucket lift has arrived. That man splicing those wires together–*that's me!"*

## Practice. Practice. Practice.

**Practicing isn't optional. It's mandatory!**

We're all familiar with the expression, "Practice makes perfect." It *doesn't!*

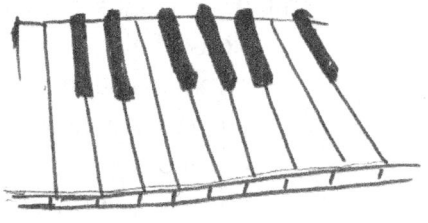

"*Perfect* practice makes perfect"–and rarely occurs.

The best attitude to have about practice is, "The road to perfection is a journey, not a destination, and it never ends."

Steve Jobs, whom many consider to be one of the best presenters ever, would practice for *weeks* before giving a presentation that introduced a new product or service at an Apple event. Bands that have been together for 30+ years still rehearse (*practice*) before performing.

Why in the world would anyone take a *Speaking* Opportunity like giving an Elevator Speech and just *wing it?*

I coach TEDx Talk speakers. The rule of thumb we have for practicing is:

One *hour* of preparation for every *minute* of presentation.

Your Elevator Speech is a mini-Presentation. If it lasts for 60 seconds, then you need to practice your speech for *at least* one hour.

Here's my BEST Tip for practicing:

Use Your iPad or computer to video record your Elevator Speech.

- The **firs**t time you play back the recording, turn the sound off and just watch.
    - Nonverbal communication trumps verbal communication.
    - Are you leaning on the table or lectern?
    - Are your eyes shifting around?
    - Are you using nonverbal cues that say you're not engaged?
- The **second** time you review the recording, turn your screen away and just listen.
    - Do you hear any filler words?
    - How is your speech rate?

- - Are you pausing too much or too little?
  - How are your pronunciation and enunciation?
- The **third** time you review the recording, *watch and listen* to the video and audio.
  - You will *see* and *hear* what the audience sees and hears.
- The **fourth** time, ask a good friend or coach to review the recording with you.
  - Have them *watch* and *listen*.
  - We all have blind spots.
  - Sometimes we're too tough on ourselves. Sometimes we miss things.
- Repeat these steps!

# Chapter 8—Tips for Networking

You've worked hard, very hard, to develop and practice your Elevator Speech. *Now* let's put it to work!

## Find an Event

Be proactive! Use social media, family members, business contacts, and others to find Elevator Speech opportunities. Let them know what type of functions you'd like to attend. Use search engines to find in-person and online events that prospects for your products and services will be attending.

Register on sites like Meetup and Eventbrite so you will receive their updates and can quickly register for an event.

Formal networking events are not the only places to meet people and present your Elevator Speech. Social functions and seminars, whether in-person or virtual, are opportunities to tell people *who* you are and *what* you do. They're also excellent opportunities to find out about products and services for yourself and to refer to others. That's what Super Connectors do!

Another way to meet new people is to join organizations in which you're interested. When they hold events, *volunteer* to help wherever needed. Working a registration table is an excellent way to see who attends, get a bit of intel on them, and put specific individuals on your prospect list to meet when your volunteer time is over.

## Networking Goals

1. Let people know *who* you are and *what* you do.
2. Discover *who* attendees are and what *they* do.
3. When possible, refer others.
4. Meet **Super Connectors**.
    - These are individuals who know everyone!
    - They're people who know someone who can help you or know somebody who knows the right person when you're looking for a particular product or service.
    - You want them to know you and what you do.
    - Because an introduction from a Super Connector is usually more valuable than introducing yourself, you want them to know you as well as your products and services. With that knowledge, they'll be prepared to introduce and refer you.
    - One possible goal is for YOU to become a Super Connector!

**Example:**
I know a business periodical publisher who meets this description.

He has been my go-to person whenever I'm looking for something related to business.

1. **Work on becoming a Super Connector.**
   Many people who attend networking events walk into a venue, look around for people they know, find someone, and spend the majority of time with that person. Sometimes their conversations are more social than business related. They'll talk until the presentation begins, sit next to each other during the program, and walk to the parking lot together when the event concludes. I call this Velcro **Networking**, and it produces no results.

   Other people walk into the same venue, find someone they don't know, then do the same thing as the person who looks for someone they know. *That's not networking either!*

   Then, the **True Networkers** arrive! They enter the venue and immediately look around to see who is attending. They search for specific people, having identified in advance the people they want to approach first, second, and so on. *They have a plan!*

## *Before* the Event-Make a Plan

Once you've chosen an event you want to attend, do some research.

- Often you'll find a list of people who are planning to attend. (Meetup.com and Eventbrite.com frequently share this information.)

- Additionally, you may see information about each attendee's company, job title, and products or services.
- After finding out who will be there, compile a list of prospects you want to meet.
- *Prioritize* your list. This step is important because you likely won't have enough time (or opportunities) to meet everyone on the list.
  - Google your prospects' names.
    - You'll be *amazed* at the information that's available. Look for things you have in common that could serve as ice breakers for conversations.
      - Sports, schools, occupations, hobbies, places lived, etc. are all things that can connect people.
      - Watch the 60's musical, *How to Succeed in Business Without Really Trying,* to see how that's done!
  - Find your prospects' profiles on LinkedIn and Facebook, and check out their connections and friends.
    - You may find someone *you* know who knows the person you want to meet.
      - Connect with your contact to see if he or she is willing to make an introduction.
      - If your contact isn't attending, you've still identified someone who knows your prospect. Use that shared relationship as part of your conversation when meeting your prospect.
        - **Example:**
          "I notice on your LinkedIn profile that you know Bill Brown. I've known Bill

for a long time. How did the two of you meet?"
- Consider sending each of your prospects a LinkedIn invitation *prior* to the event.
    - **Example:**
    "I noticed you'll be attending the office supplier event next Friday and wanted to connect with you on LinkedIn. Let's get together at the event because I have a prospect in mind for you and want to make an introduction."
    Do additional research and checks.
- If you're attending an event in person, get there well before the kick-off.
    - Know where the event will be held and how to get there.
    - Check on parking.
- If you're joining the event online, what platform will you need to use?
    - Make sure you have the proper software and credentials to access the event; if necessary, update your software *before* logging in.
    - Check your camera, lighting, and background.

## *During* the Event—Work Your Plan

- In Person: Arrive Early!
    - The host or event planner is always a great person and connector to meet.

- Check out locations in advance for possible one-on-one conversations (e.g., near restrooms, refreshment setups, food courts, and break areas).
- Find out if a roster with contact information will be provided.
- Take a supply of business cards with you.
  - Have your current contact information on your phone to easily share with people who prefer electronics.
- Keep your prioritized list of prospects handy. Start looking for the people you want to meet as well as personal contacts who can make introductions.
  - If you see someone you want to meet who is already engaged in a conversation, *don't* interrupt. *Do* make eye contact to signal interest in introducing yourself.
  - If it looks like they're going to be having an extended conversation, move on down your list.
  - You won't meet everyone, but you should be able to meet the people you consider most important.

***NO SWEAT Elevator Speech!***

- Remember: you don't want to spend *major* time (theirs or yours) on *minor* possibilities.
- Use your practiced Elevator Speech to *dis*qualify people.

o Focus on people who signal interest, and exchange paper or electronic business cards. If possible, invite prospects to meet with you later and set a time and date for a conversation.

- On the backs of business cards you collect, make quick notes for setting up conversations and anything else pertinent to *you* or *them*, such as potential referrals.
- Code the business cards you collect using numbers, colors, or symbols to prioritize them for follow-up.

- Online: Arrive Early!

o When I lead events, I usually log on at least ten minutes before starting time. Other organizers often do the same, and these are good people with whom to start networking. They can give you a heads-up about the agenda and other attendees.

- Again, find out if a roster of attendees and their contact information will be provided.
- Inquire if they'll be asking people to introduce themselves. They may assume everyone knows each other. However, occupations change.

o The chat function of virtual meeting platforms is a great place to ask for contact information and quickly ask and answer a few questions.

- Have your contact information ready to share in a PDF file so you can quickly upload the file in the chat window.

*Fred E. Miller*

# Delivering Your Elevator Speech One-on-One During the Event

*What follows is a typical scenario for meeting a person during the networking portion of an event.*

I approach a person I want to meet, extend my hand for a handshake (or fist bump), and say,

**First Floor**: "Hi! I'm Fred."

Prospect: "Nice to meet you, Fred. What do you do?"

**Second Floor**: "I'm a speaker, coach, and author."

Prospect: "Oh, what have you written?"

**Third Floor**: "Thanks for asking. I've written two books: *NO SWEAT Public Speaking!* and *NO SWEAT Elevator Speech!*"

Prospect: "Interesting. Tell me more."

(Since my prospect has shown an interest, I go to the next floor of my Elevator Speech.)

**Fourth Floor**: "Businesses, individuals, and organizations *hire* me *because* they want to improve their networking, public speaking, and presentation skills." (If my prospect continues to show interest, verbally or nonverbally, I continue.)

**Fifth Floor:** "They do that because they know *Speaking* Opportunities are *Business, Career,* and *Leadership* Opportunities.

(As long as my prospect's still showing interest and hasn't stopped me, I'll keep going.)

### NO SWEAT Elevator Speech!

**Sixth Floor:** "They also know we perceive *really good speakers* as *Experts!* We like to work with Experts–*right?*

(Since my prospect is still "on the elevator," I tell them *What I Deliver*.)

**Seventh Floor**: "I show them how to develop, practice, and deliver *outstanding* presentations with–**NO SWEAT!**"

(In this scenario, I move forward to the top floor where I ASK...,)

**Eighth Floor:** "Enough about me. How does *your* company handle internal and external Presentation Skills Training?

Networking one-on-one is also an opportunity to use an *EXPRESS* Elevator Speech.

### Example:

After exchanging names at the event, and perhaps giving me *his* or *her* Elevator Speech, the person asks me, "What do you do, Fred?"

I respond by saying,

"Thanks for asking, Bob. I'm going to answer your question by asking one.

Have you ever been to an event where you're watching and listening to a speaker and think...

"Wow! This guy is good, *really* good. He's articulate, very entertaining, and obviously has a passion for what he's doing. I'm getting a *lot* out of his presentation. *Gosh*, I wish *I* could do that. (P-A-U-S-E) I'm the guy people hire to develop, practice, and deliver *outstanding* presentations like that."

My prospect might suggest that we get together to learn more. If so, we'll exchange contact information and set a date and time to meet in the near future.

If I get a negative response, I'll *Go for NO* and add,

"Everyone who hires me believes speaking opportunities are *Business*, *Career*, and *Leadership* opportunities.

You probably don't know anyone who wants to improve their public speaking and presentation skills, *do you?*"

At this point, my prospect either indicates we should talk in the future, offers a referral, or signals it's time for both of us to move on.

## Have a Getaway Plan

Unfortunately, some people attend networking events to socialize rather than to meet new prospects. They have no agenda except to enjoy themselves. They may approach you and would be content to spend all the allotted time with you.

Networking time is limited, and you want it to be as productive as possible. One parameter is to avoid spending *major* time on *minor* possibilities. Have several plans to get away from people once you've *dis*qualified them.

### *Suggestions:*

When you realize someone is not a good prospect and the chances for a referral are minimal, it's time to move on. Say, "Excuse me. I set a goal for this event to meet ten new people.

You're number ___. Let's continue this conversation another time." Ask to exchange business cards, make a note on theirs, shake hands or bump fists, and find the next person on your prospect list.

If you realize that you want to move on, look around for someone on your prospect list and tell the person you're talking with presently, "Excuse me. I just spotted someone I've *got* to see today. Here's my card. Please give me yours. Let's continue this conversation another time."

## Delivering Your Elevator Speech to a Group During the Event

Especially for smaller groups, before a program begins and after welcoming remarks, the leader will announce: "Before we get started, let's go around the room. When it's your turn, stand and tell us *who* you are and *what* you do. Give us your *Elevator Speech*. Let's keep it to a minute or less. Who wants to go first?"

As you'll recall from an earlier chapter, the Law of Primacy and Recency says an audience best remembers the first and last things a speaker says and does.

This phenomenon also applies to Elevator Speeches, particularly the *order* of presentations. If you can be the *first* or *last* person to deliver your Elevator Speech, you increase the odds that an audience will remember you and your message. Speaking last is slightly better than going first, but speaking order is rarely something you can control. Raise your hand high when you hear the question, "Who wants to be first?"

When delivering your Elevator Speech, use all the verbal and nonverbal elements of communication discussed previously to demonstrate *confidence* in your *competence*.

- Smile!
- Clearly enunciate and pronounce your words
- Use emphasis
- Vary your speech rate
- Insert pauses strategically
- Look an interested person in the eye, finish your thought, then look at someone else
- Stand up straight
- Avoid fidgeting

## Develop a *Post*-Networking Event Plan

You've put a great deal of time, effort, and (perhaps) money into developing a great Elevator Speech, finding an event, and networking with prospects.

You are *not* finished! As Abraham Lincoln said, "Things will come to those who sit and wait, but only things left by those who hustle." It's time to *hustle!*

- Debrief
    - That same evening or the following day, debrief yourself about the event.
    - How well did you deliver your Elevator Speech?
    - What did you do well?
        - Where can you improve?
    - How many of your prospects and Super Connectors did you meet?

- Follow-up
    - Email or call everyone who agreed to a follow-up conversation.
    - Even with people who aren't good prospects but who exchanged contact information with you, send a brief "Nice meeting you!" email to remind them '*who* you are and *what* you do.' In the future, they may need or want to refer you.
    - Enter all names and contact information in your database or Contact Relationship Management (CRM) program.
        - You'll need this information for future drip marketing.
    - Keep in touch via regular emails, phone calls, and even text messages.
- Referrals
    - Can you think of people and businesses that are prospects for products and services offered by people you met?
    - If so, have a plan for introducing them via phone, email, or face-to-face.
    - Remember the "Law of Reciprocity" and the benefits of being a Super Connector.

*Start Searching for the Next Opportunity to Deliver Your Elevator Speech!*

# Chapter 9—Fear of Public Speaking

An Elevator Speech is a mini-Presentation. Delivering one is called **Public Speaking**. One reason many people struggle with Elevator Speeches is **Fear of Public Speaking.**

You can have the greatest Elevator Speech ever, but Fear of Public Speaking can raise its ugly head and sabotage your ability to deliver it well.

Survey after survey agrees this fear is one of the most common phobias. Up to 75% of the population experiences it to one degree or another. Some feel a slight nervousness at the very thought of public speaking, while others experience full-on panic and fear. There are even people who fear public speaking more than dying.

There's even a word for Fear of Public Speaking—**Glossophobia**, which comes from the Greek language: *Glōssa,* tongue, and *Phobos,* dread or fear. The important thing to note is that Glossophobia is a WORD, *not* a disease, and it *can be lessened!*

In my research, I have discovered that Fear of Public Speaking is an equal opportunity fear. It doesn't care about your age, education, or occupation. I have coached doctors, lawyers, students, entrepreneurs, psychologists, and many others.

In most of my keynote talks, workshops, and coaching, I include a discussion about this fear. It holds many people back both personally and professionally. In the following section, I'll cover WHY we experience Fear of Public Speaking. In the next chapter, I'll give you Nuggets to Lessen that Fear.

## WHY Do People Fear Public Speaking?

Whenever I'm asked this question, my first response is, *Why not?*

Think about it. Most communication is one-on-one, and many of these conversations take place by phone. We don't see the other person, and he or she isn't looking at us

Additionally, communication is increasingly conducted via text, email, and direct messaging. When we use these media, we neither *see* nor *hear* each other.

Given this fact of modern-day life, it's not unusual for someone standing in front often, twenty, thirty, or more sets of eyeballs to be *un*comfortable. For many, doing so is like stepping into a spotlight they didn't choose!

We rarely speak publicly and doing so puts us out of our comfort zones. Stepping outside our comfort zones, whatever the activity is, makes us *un*comfortable.

## Imposter Syndrome

Some people experience Fear of Public Speaking because of **Imposter Syndrome**, which is doubting one's abilities and feeling like a fraud.

High achievers who find it difficult to accept their accomplishments are affected disproportionately.

Young people who have older workers as subordinates are sometimes victims of this phenomenon, as are women, minorities, and individuals with low self-esteem.

As speakers, they may think the audience is wondering,

- *Why* am *I* in this position?
- *Who* did *I* know to get the job?
- *Really? They* do *that?*

My response is, "*You* are in that position because others who are putting *their* own reputations on the line decided *you* are the best person for the job. They stand by their decision. You should accept and embrace the decision, too!

## Fear of Failure

Fear of Public Speaking goes hand in hand with **Fear of Failure**. Who likes to fail? *Most don't.*

The truth is we should all *welcome* failure. Failing is one of the best ways to learn. Here's a typical "failure scenario":

- Fail
- Get upset
- Figure out what went wrong
- Think of ways to fix the problem
- Try those fixes
- See what works
- You *learned something new!*

One formula for success is: Fail *early* and fail *often.*

Bill Gates said, "If you get it right the *first* time, you don't give it a *second* thought."

That makes sense, *doesn't it?*

## Reasons Behind Our Fear of Public Speaking

In addition to feeling out of our comfort zones, there are legitimate reasons to experience Fear of Public Speaking.

### *If you don't know your topic*

Don't get in front of an audience and speak about a topic you know little about.

You'll never know everything about a subject, but you should know enough that you're comfortable delivering the information to others, including people who are knowledgeable about the subject matter.

### *If you don't know how to structure a presentation*

We've all experienced speakers who talked–talked–talked, didn't say much, and were almost impossible to follow. Sometimes they would repeat things and get off topic.

*Don't* be one of those speakers!

Like a great cake, there's a recipe for developing and delivering a great Elevator Speech or presentation.

You now have templates (recipes) for Elevator Speeches. Develop several and use them.

### *If you haven't practiced*

Practicing is *not* optional! (More on this later!)

## Other Factors that Can Bring on Fear of Public Speaking

### Number of people in the audience

I often hear, "I have no problem talking one-on-one or even to several people at a time, but...."

As audience size increases, so does Fear of Public Speaking.

Here's an analogy: Fear of Heights.

I don't mind standing on a step stool or step ladder.

Climbing an extension ladder that reaches the gutters on my two-story home—*Yikes!*

### Specific individuals in the audience

I know a financial planner who regularly speaks to large audiences with no fear. However, if his boss or colleagues are seated in front, he is All Sweat!

### Having to ask the audience to do something

Some speakers experience no anxiety when speaking to a full room. However, if part of their talk includes asking the audience to do something (e.g., write a check, take a pledge, or give a referral), their nervous tension increases.

## What-Ifs?

We often talk to ourselves. When it comes to public speaking, some of that self-talk is negative.

- *WHAT IF* who I am and what I do is boring?

- *WHAT IF* I do a lousy job of telling people what I do?
- WHAT IF people who hear my Elevator Speech don't like me?
- *WHAT IF* I forget part of the message?
- *WHAT IF* I fail to deliver the speech perfectly?
- *WHAT IF* I get no reaction or worse, a negative response from the audience?
- *WHAT IF* people look confused after I deliver my speech?

Worrying about the WHAT-IFs can negatively impact your Elevator Speech. **STOP doing it**!

Keep in mind, your audience is more concerned about themselves. Who you are and what you do is not their main focus, but it should be yours! Present your Elevator Speech well, and they will GET IT!

Let's move on to lessening a Fear of Public Speaking!

# Chapter 10—Nuggets to Lessen Fear of Public Speaking

### Nervousness

Those Butterflies we feel in our stomachs from Fear of Public Speaking–we *don't* want to get rid of them completely. The objective is to channel that energy into our Elevator Speeches. A presentation or Elevator Speech without energy is b-o-r-i-n-g! (Ever sit through one? *Yech!)*

Toastmasters says, "Teach those butterflies to fly in formation!" *That*'s great advice.

### *Never* Tell Your Audience You Are Afraid!

When it's their turn to deliver an Elevator Speech, I've seen and heard people stand up and promptly announce, "I have a terrible Fear of Public Speaking. I hate doing this and didn't prepare well. Here's my Elevator Speech: _____."

Because they set themselves up for failure and the audience expects it, their Elevator Speeches are *under*-whelming. The negative mini-introductions they give before explaining *who* they are and *what* they do become a self-fulfilling prophecy.

*Don't do that!* If you do, your audience will be looking for you to mess up, and you won't disappoint them.

## You Don't Have to Be Perfect

If you're in a theater production, it's your turn to speak, and you forget your script–*you're in trouble.*

If you're in a marching band and suddenly realize you are moving in a *different* direction than the rest of the group–*you're in trouble.*

If you deliver your Elevator Speech differently than you scripted and practiced it–NO ONE KNOWS! They don't know you messed up and, unless you tell them, *they will never know.*

That's one of the nice things about Elevator Speeches and Public Speaking. *These types of presentations don't have to be perfect!* In fact, if they're "too perfect," you come off like some kind of robot. Presentations and Elevator Speeches should be delivered in a conversational manner. A bit of "struggling" humanizes your delivery.

## Be Audience-Centered

Successful businesses are Customer-Centered. They focus on their customers' wants and needs.

Fulfilling them makes the company successful.
- The medical community is Patient-Centered.
- Educators are Student-Centered.
- The hospitality industry is Guest-Centered.

### NO SWEAT Elevator Speech!

To be successful in delivering presentations and Elevator Speeches, you need to be **Audience-Centered.**

*It's all about your Audience, not about you as the speaker!*

No one comes to an event to hear your mini-Presentation. They come to learn something and network. *You* are not the reason they are attending.

If you focus on yourself rather than your audience, *you're in trouble–BIG Trouble*–whether you're speaking to 1 or 100 people. You start thinking about *you* and *your* Elevator Speech.

- How do I look?
- Am I talking too quickly?
- Am I talking too slowly?
- Am I mumbling?
- Am I forgetting something?

Being Audience-Centered is one of the Laws of Presentations, and it applies to Elevator Speeches, too. Understand it–Believe it–Practice it! The quality of your presentation will go *up* and your anxiety will go *down*.

Speaking of the Audience, they are *cheering* for you! No one wants to embarrass themselves delivering *their* Elevator Speech, and they want *you* to be successful. They *want* to know *who* you are and *what* you do.

No one is listening and wanting you to mess up so they can diss you on Facebook and LinkedIn. If you do make a mistake, they feel for you and share your embarrassment, but they don't think any less of you. They can *see* themselves doing the same thing.

I always ask my audiences, "Are any of you waiting for me to make a mistake so you can jump on social media and criticize me? Maybe write something like 'What a terrible speaker! Don't waste your time asking for his Elevator Speech?'"

*NO!* You're glad *I'm* the one who's talking and *not* you, right?"

Bottom Line: Focus on the *Audience*, not yourself.

## All Audiences Are Not the Same

Just because something you said or did while delivering your Elevator Speech got great laughter from one group doesn't mean you'll get the same reaction from every audience.

That's the way it is. Don't let it throw you off your game. When your Elevator Speech wows once but flops the next time, do a postmortem and see if the difference had anything to do with your message, subject, audience, or occasion. Was your Elevator Speech universally understood, industry specific, or germane to specific audiences only? If so, that's an opportunity to fine tune your message.

Knowing this can happen prepares you for diverse audiences. Prepare, practice, and do your best to always be Audience-Centered.

For many people, the discomfort associated with delivering an Elevator Speech will lessen as they speak to *different* groups on a *regular* basis.

Giving speeches to dissimilar groups is important. I know people who overcame their speaking anxiety and got comfortable giving talks at their regular Toastmasters meetings. However, when they got in front of an unfamiliar audience—*Whoa!* The experience was different, *very* different.

## Arrive at Events Early So You Can Meet & Greet

It's amazing how much easier it is to deliver your Elevator Speech to an audience where you've already met the individuals who compose it.

Just introducing yourself with an outstretched hand (maybe), fist, or elbow and telling them, "I'm Fred. I'm glad you're here!" makes a *huge* difference in your anxiety level.

I'm usually one of the first to arrive at an event. I want to greet as many people as possible.

If you do so, too, other attendees will appreciate your introduction and feel a connection to you. You'll better relate to everyone when you tell them *who* you are and *what* you do.

*Fred E. Miller*

## Find Friendly Faces in Your Audience

There will be people in your audience who are "loving" your Elevator Speech! They'll be listening to every word and soaking up each "floor" as you deliver it.

These folks will energize you! Find one such person, make eye contact, and talk directly to him or her until you've finished a floor. Then, move on to another friendly face. Do the same with this person and continue until you're finished.

If you see people with blank stares on their faces, don't despair. They probably like what they're seeing and hearing. However, not everyone expresses likes and dislikes in the same manner as you. Don't worry about them. Simply move on and keep looking for friendly faces, positive body language, or pleasant facial expressions indicating that these folks are *GETTING IT!*

You'll never make a great connection with the entire audience. Everyone brings "stuff" to the event that is going on in their lives, which can influence their attention to your presentation. Perhaps, they are late completing a project, have problems at home, or are thinking of their next vacation. If you find someone giving you a look of dissatisfaction, anger, or sleepiness–*Move On!* Not everyone will *GET IT!* and that's OK!

## Have a "Spare Tire"

When you're embarking on a cross-country road trip, a great stress reliever is knowing your trunk contains a good spare tire, lug wrench, and functioning car jack.

The analogy holds true for delivering great Elevator Speeches. Handwritten notes or a **Mindmap** (i.e., visual representation of your speech) on an index card in your pocket gives you a sense of security.

If you suddenly get anxious about delivering your Elevator Speech, you can use your "spare tire." You can preface reaching for your index card by saying, "I've been working on a new Elevator Speech. Please share your feedback." Such an introduction to your Elevator Speech makes it OK to use your "cheat sheet." No one will think less of you, and you will deliver your message as intended.

Using props or visual aids related to *what* you do can also be helpful in reminding you what to say. Holding a hammer, stethoscope, or book can remind you of something specific in your Elevator Speech and help you make that point with your audience.

## Deep Breathing Exercises

Please try this exercise:

Count to three, take a deep breath, and sigh! Really *sigh*.

You feel better already, *don't you?*

We sigh when we're upset or angry. Doing so eases that stress.

**Deep Breathing** is *formalized sighing*. There are several different ways to practice Deep Breathing, and I encourage you to explore a few.

One very simple Deep Breathing exercise that works for me is to breathe in deeply to the count of six and exhale completely to the count of eight.

Practice this exercise *before* attending a function where you'll have a *Speaking* Opportunity to deliver your Elevator Speech. Experiment and find a method that works for you.

## Get a Good Night's Sleep

When we're thoroughly rested, we work better. Our mind is sharper, and our performance is stronger. Don't underestimate this fact and get plenty of sleep before attending a function where you'll have a *Speaking* Opportunity to give your Elevator Speech.

## Keep Your Body in Good Physical Condition

I'm a walker, and walking gets my endorphins going and my mind functioning at its best. I develop and practice some of the best parts of my Elevator Speeches when going for a power walk. (I always take my phone with me on walks and use it to capture things to add or fine tune.)

Any kind of regular exercise will keep your mind sharp and your body healthy.

A proper diet, regular exercise, and healthy habits are good ways to help you look and feel your best when delivering your Elevator Speech. Your energy level goes *up* and your anxiety goes *down*. It's easier to project a positive and confident image to your audience when your body and mind feel good!

## Meditation

Napoleon Hill, an American self-help author best known for his book *Think and Grow Rich,* is famous for saying, "Whatever the mind of man can conceive, he can achieve."

In your mind's eye before an event, *picture yourself* delivering your Elevator Speech with confidence. *Picture your audience* giving you eye contact, leaning in, and listening attentively. Picture them *GETTING IT!*

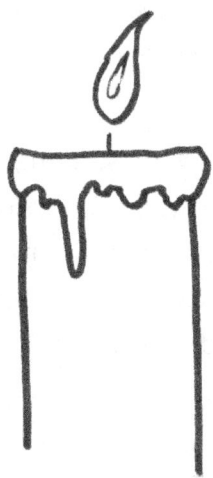

Combine your meditation with **Positive Affirmations** in the present tense, such as

"I've got this!"

"I'm at ease, look good, and am projecting confidence in my competence."

"My audience is watching, listening, and *GETTING* my Elevator Speech."

And, if meditation doesn't work, try...

## Medication, Hypnosis, Psychotherapy, or Tapping

Sometimes the chemistry of our bodies makes it almost impossible to work on the fundamentals of an Elevator Speech because our Fear of Public Speaking is so great.

There are prescription medications called **Beta Blockers** that can help. They reduce anxiety so a person can more easily work on the Content and Delivery of a presentation or Elevator Speech.

There's nothing wrong with securing a prescription! I once coached an extremely motivated physician who couldn't move forward with her speaking until her anxiety was controlled. She sought out another doctor who prescribed the proper medicine and dosage, and she's doing great!

Some people seek and receive help from **Hypnosis**. Others find that **Psychotherapy** can get to the root of the fear and relieve it.

For yet others, a form of acupuncture that uses the fingertips to stimulate energy points on the body, called Emotional Freedom Technique (EFT) or **Tapping,** can lessen Fear of Public Speaking.

Important: If your fear is preventing you from moving forward, *find something that works!*

## Cotton Mouth

**Cotton Mouth** is no fun!

Your mouth is as dry as, well, cotton! It's no fun to experience, and it's difficult to talk with this condition. Feeling unable to speak intensifies anxiety. The mere thought of delivering your Elevator Speech and suddenly experiencing Cotton Mouth can bring on the jitters.

Being nervous is one of several things that can lead to Cotton Mouth. Certain prescription drugs (e.g., antihistamines) and dry air are others. Caffeine can cause further dryness and exacerbate your dry mouth symptoms. You can still drink warm beverages like coffee or tea, but decaffeinated versions would be better for you.

Cotton Mouth is an uncomfortable feeling that only gets worse and adds to anxiety if you cannot relieve it.

Always have room-temperature water available. Liquids that are too hot or too cold will adversely affect your vocal cords.

Another way to get relief is to place a small lozenge between your cheek and gum. Experiment with this option *before* giving your actual Elevator Speech to get the *flavor* of how it works.

Lemon or menthol flavors are best because cherry can make your mouth look like it's bleeding!

Rinses and sprays for dry mouth are alternative remedies. However, as with lozenges, test them *before* using them in a "real-life" situation.

Chewing gum is NOT a good idea. Chewing gum looks like you're...well, chewing gum...and that can be a distraction.

## Join Toastmasters

Toastmasters is an international organization. The latest figures reveal membership is approaching 357,000 people in more than 16,600 clubs in 143 countries.

One of the most valuable benefits of being a member is the nurturing environment where everyone truly wants to help the other members.

Toastmasters offers two tracks: Speaking and Leadership. You can practice very specific skills in each track and achieve increasing levels of competence. Both tracks are excellent ways to learn and hone skills that will benefit you forever. The ability to speak in front of groups and lead meetings are tools you need along the career path of life.

Before joining a club, my suggestion is to visit at least three or four clubs in your area. Each club has a flavor of its own. Some are very regimented, adhere to Robert's Rules of Order, and are strict about the way things are done during meetings. Other clubs thrive at the opposite end of the spectrum–where things are a little more relaxed. (Many exist somewhere between these two extremes.)

There are also 'company' clubs in large corporations as well as clubs that are specific to certain interests, such as humor or professional speaking.

Check out **https://www.toastmasters.org** for great information and a listing of clubs in your area.

## Take Courses

In many cities, community colleges and private companies offer public speaking courses. Explore a few and ask for outlines of courses offered. Find out who the instructors are and investigate their credentials.

You can also find many online programs. Check out several and read their reviews before making a purchase.

## Hire a Coach!

Athletes have coaches. Actors have coaches. Business executives have coaches.

**The greatest investment you can ever make is in yourself.**

Hiring a great professional-presentation coach is a solid investment because:

1. They can greatly reduce your learning curve.
   - Yes, you can get better by attending classes, watching videos, and reading books.
   - However, a coach, especially one who also speaks professionally, is *invaluable!*
     o They have "been there and done that."
     o They have made many mistakes and can dramatically lessen the ones you might make.
2. You have their *undivided* attention, and you aren't one of many participants in a classroom or auditorium, or on a webinar.
   - The feedback and advice they'll give is specifically for *you* during each coaching session, and not a "one-size-fits-all" piece of advice.
3. They will "tell it like it is."
   - Your coach has no agenda. You are paying for their honesty, and they will be truthful in both their praise and critiques.
   - Friends and family may not be the best at advising you, especially if public speaking isn't their area of expertise.
4. They will hold you accountable and use a structure to get your Elevator Speech presentation skills to where you want them to be.
5. They can serve as a sounding board for new ideas about topics and delivery.
   - The whole is greater than the sum of its parts when it comes to working on the components of a talk.
   - "Let's talk through this" is a phrase that's often used in coaching.
6. Once they've gained your confidence, you can talk to them in confidence. This is important.

- I've had many clients tell me about their fears of facing an audience when they've told nobody else.
- I've also had ideas thrown at me that my clients thought others would find nonsensical–and would ridicule them for even suggesting.

7. One important quality of a good coach is that they will listen and ask questions so you can hear yourself respond.

Bottom Line:

No matter what skill you want to improve, you can get it to a higher level more quickly by hiring a professional coach. This certainly applies to improving your Elevator Speeches as well as your public speaking and presentation skills.

The *Return on Investment* of hiring a coach can be *Phenomenal!*

BTW, *I do that!* Contact me: **Fred@NoSweatPublicSpeaking.com**

## Fear Busters

Frances Cahill, a public-speaking coach in Queensland, Australia, suggests using the following ten **Fear Busters** to prepare for a presentation. I liked them so much that I asked her permission to share them in this book, and she generously agreed.

1. Power
    - Stand feet apart, elbows into your side, palms upwards and clenched.
    - Bend your knees and grunt from your belly.
2. Stance
    - Stand like a Superhero: Wonder Woman or Superman with feet apart, hands on hips and elbows outwards.

3. Smile
   - If you smile, you are tricking your brain and your body. Try the Mona (or Milton) Lisa smile.
   - Try out a grin. Make it a slow drawling smile.
   - Practice any smile and feel the muscle stretch.
4. Smell
   - Take a moment to smell the scent of your perfume or aftershave.
   - Remember a smell that brings back good memories.
   - Take a flower with you and smell it as you get up to speak.
5. Imagine
   - Stop for a moment and see yourself speaking fluently and confidently.
   - Hear a favorite song in your mind.
   - Hear the sound of applause.
   - See the words "I CAN DO THIS" rolling across your mind.
6. Talisman
   - Take a physical object with you to touch—a necklace, watch, tie clip, cufflinks, or button.
   - Rest your hand on a chair back.
   - Place your hand on the lectern.
   - Touch your phone–to turn it off.
7. Breathe
   - Never forget this one.
   - Just breathe when you first feel the signs of panic rising.
   - Let out the breath you are holding.
   - Count the length of your breath.
   - Feel the air go through your nose.
   - Push the air out through your mouth.
8. Ground
   - Start from the ground up to stand or walk.

- Feel the floor through your shoes.
- Wiggle your toes.
- Stand up from a chair and move it aside.

9. Voice
    - Warm yours up! Your performance and presentation have many elements.
    - Move your mouth and listen to your humming.
    - Try a tongue twister–"picked a peck of pickled peppers."
    - Sing or say a short phrase–"Mary had a little lamb."
    - Say your name quickly three times.
10. Count
    - Backwards from 100 in 7s.
    - Number of chairs by 3.
    - Windows in the room.
    - Panels on the back wall.

## Practice! Practice! Practice!

Every four years the Olympics are held. Does anyone think that great athletes just "Show Up" for their big games, matches, or meets?

Of course not! Many have left friends and families, and they have sacrificed years of their lives to the hard work of preparing for those prestigious games.

How about professional singers, actors, and musicians? Do you think they just "Show Up" for their important shows, plays, or concerts?

*No-o-o!*

Practice! Practice! Practice!

*Fred E. Miller*

Rehearse! Rehearse! Rehearse!

Even bands that have been together for more than thirty years will rehearse before going on stage.

Why would anyone think you can simply stand up at an event and Wing It when delivering your Elevator Speech?

Obvious answer—*You Can't!*

You Must Practice!
- Practice your Elevator Speech using an audio recorder.
    - Is your voice loud and clear?
    - Are you speaking distinctly or mumbling some of your words?
    - How well are you pacing your delivery?
- Practice in front of a mirror.
    - Look yourself in the eye as you speak.
- Practice in your "mind's eye."
    - Picture the audience being interested in your presentation.
    - Picture yourself being calm and collected in your thoughts and delivery.
- Practice in front of friends and family.
    - Ask for honest feedback.
    - Hearing, "Great talk!" doesn't help you improve.
    - Ask them to tell you three *specific* things they like and why—*as well as* three "opportunities" for improvement.
- As I shared with you in Chapter 7, my BEST tip for practicing is to use your iPad or computer and make both an audio and video recording of yourself presenting your Elevator Speech.

- Review the audio and video several times.
  - *Look* at your nonverbal communication.
  - *Listen* to your verbal communication.
  - Have a 'coach' review the audio and video with you.
  - Make another set of recordings and repeat the same steps.

Practice and tweak to consistently improve your Content and Delivery.

I cannot overemphasize the importance of practicing. However, you want to avoid sounding mechanical when you deliver your Elevator Speech. Struggle a bit. Appear to be thinking about your next sentence.

**Rehearse–Rehearse–Rehearse** so much that when you deliver your Elevator Speech, the audience will think it is *Un*rehearsed!

## My Golden Nugget!

If you only *GET* one idea from this book about improving your Elevator Speeches and lessening your Fear of Public Speaking, *this* is it–

*Speak!*
*Speak! Speak! Speak!*

If you want to be a master baker—*Bake!*

If you want to be a competitive swimmer—*Swim!*

If you want to be a great speaker—*Speak!*

## "The Learning is in the Doing!"

You can do all the intellectualizing you want about delivering a great Elevator Speech:

- Read books and articles.
- Watch videos.
- Listen to audio recordings.
- Observe others delivering their Elevator Speeches.
- Practice in your mind's eye.

## The Real Learning is in the Doing!

There's no easy way, and nothing beats the real thing.

*Deliver your Elevator Speech*

- In front of friends and family.
- To Chambers of Commerce.
- To Lions Clubs, Rotaries, Optimists, and other organizations where they regularly have outside speakers.

*Do it* as often as you can!

*What's the worst thing that could happen?*

### NO SWEAT Elevator Speech!

- The baker's cake falls.
- The swimmer comes in last.
- The speaker bombs.
- Big Deal!
- Who Cares!

*It's a drop in the ocean of your life. It's nothing!*

Each time you deliver your Elevator Speech, you'll learn something and improve. When results start coming in, you'll see your hard work paying off. You'll also feel better about yourself for having accomplished something that most struggle with.

# Chapter 11—*Failure* Gets a Bad Rap

Have you ever failed? *Of course,* you have.

Now, think of a specific time and event where you failed.

**Question:**
Did you learn more from that failure or from something that gave you the exact outcome you wanted the first time you tried?

Personally, if I get something right the first time–it's probably dumb luck. When that happens, I rarely make a mental note saying, "If this happens, again, I'll do that." The incident doesn't teach me anything new. I'll bet your experiences are similar, *correct?*

Bill Gates said, "If you get it right the *first* time, you don't give it a *second* thought."

Research shows that we learn *far* more from our failures than our successes. *Failing is a really good thing!* The letters in **FAIL** stand for:

**F**irst

**A**ttempt

**I**n

**L**earning

*Why*, then, are we so afraid of failing?

Perhaps, it's the word—Failure. We take the word personally because we often define it as

- Lack of success
- An unsuccessful person

I propose that we forget the word, Failure, and substitute the word, **Experiment**. One definition of Experiment is "to conduct a test to learn something or to discover if something works or is true." We rarely expect experiments to reveal the results we are seeking, right?

There's a story about Thomas Edison completing more than 10,000 experiments before inventing the light bulb. At the time, a reporter asked him, "How does it feel to have failed more than 10,000 times in your search for developing an electric light bulb?"

The genius inventor replied, "I have not failed. I've just found 10,000 ways that don't work." If it hadn't been for his tenacity and *never-give-up* attitude, he would have never reached his goal. *That's* the mindset we should have, *isn't it?*

### NO SWEAT Elevator Speech!

**One proven formula for Success is:**

Fail *Early*.
Fail *Often*.
Fail *Quickly*.
Sometimes, *Fail BIG!*

Go BIG or Go Home!

Failure gets a Bad Rap. We should be *embracing* it!

I'm fond of the great basketball player Michael Jordan's take on Failure. He said,

> "*I've missed more than 9,000 shots in my career.*
>
> *I've lost almost 300 games.*
>
> *Twenty-six times I've been trusted to take the game winning shot–and missed.*
>
> *I've failed over and over and over again in my life.*
>
> *That is why I succeed."*
>
> *The only real failure is not failing."*

Think about it!

**When–Why–Where**

I remember a time when one of my grandsons, Carson, was visiting our home. At eleven months of age, he wasn't walking yet, but he was *trying!*

If you've ever observed a baby learning to walk, you know what a great lesson in persistence it is. The child's determination reminds me of the great quote from the *Apollo 13* movie, "Failure is not an option!"

Carson pulled himself up to a standing position using a coffee table in our living room. I watched him get his balance. He kept his hands on the table and moved his legs gingerly, side to side. He let go with one hand and gave us a big, proud smile. Then, he let go with the other hand and stood on his own for a second or two, then–*boom!* He fell.

He sat on the floor for a moment or two without crying, then pulled himself up again. I watched another big smile come over his face as he got his balance, moved a step or two sideways, let go with one hand, then the other and–fell!

As he sat on the floor smiling, he....

Well, you can see where I'm going with this story, can't you?

***When–Why–Where*** did we decide that we will not *immediately* pull ourselves up–*and try again* if we fall?

### I *Guarantee*

The *worst* Elevator Speech you'll *ever* give will be far better than the one you *never* give.

### That bears repeating!

The *worst* Elevator Speech you'll *ever* give will be far better than the one you *never* give!

# Chapter 12—Conclusion

**Let's review what we've learned about Elevator Speeches.**

In its simplest form, an Elevator Speech is a personal infomercial that clearly and concisely tells others *who* you are and *what* you do.

An Elevator Speech is a mini-Presentation. Like all presentations, they have two components: Content and Delivery.
- **Content** can be developed using the Elevator Speech Templates. They are available here:
  - **NoSweatPublicSpeaking.com/go/FreeElevator SpeechTemplate**
- **Delivery** involves presenting the "Floors" to others.

## Goals of an Elevator Speech

### *The Ultimate Goal is a conversation.*

You want a conversation with someone who has a sincere interest in your product or service.

They want to know:
- How you work
- What it costs
    - If discounts are available
    - If financing is available
- How long it takes

- When they can start if they hire you
- If you offer guarantees

## The Immediate Goal is Understanding.

People who hear your Elevator Speech should–*GET IT!* Unless they know *who* you are and *what* you do, you will *not* be hired or referred.

Your listeners are *sorting and sifting* the information you're conveying and then deciding the next step they will take:
- Contact you immediately for more information
- File your information for the future if a need arises
- Refer you to someone who needs your offerings

*Everyone* who hears your Elevator Speech should know *exactly who* you are and *what* you do.
- To achieve this goal, you Elevator Speech must be:
  o Clear, Concise, and Consistent.
  o You can have several Elevator Speeches, each of which is aimed at specific groups.
- To test your Elevator Speech for clarity, try this:
  o Invite someone who *doesn't* know *who* you are and *what* you do (Person #1) to ask someone who HAS heard your Elevator Speech (Person #2) to share this information about you.
  o After hearing this information, Person #1 should know *who* you are and *what* you do and should be able to tell others.

## Another Important Goal is to Dis-qualify.

- Everyone is not a prospect for your products and services. Think about it for a moment. Do you buy everything that's offered to you?

- Don't spend *major* time on *minor* possibilities. *Everyone's* time, including yours, is valuable. Use it productively and be respectful of other people's time.

### Remember: NO Selling!
- Selling will come later, if it will occur.

## Delivery

You now have "Floor-by-Floor" templates for developing, practicing, and delivering your Elevator Speeches.

Once you complete, modify, and practice them, you'll have confidence in your competence and will be able to deliver great ones.

**Delivery** of your Elevator Speech is almost more important than the speech itself.

You can have the greatest Elevator Speech ever, but if you fail to deliver it confidently and in a manner that educates, entertains, and explains *who* you are and *what* you do, your audience will never *GET IT!*

Be mindful that your Elevator Speech has two components: **Verbal** and **Nonverbal**, with your nonverbal communication outweighing the words you speak.

Make certain the two components are in sync.

If not, people will believe what you're conveying nonverbally.

WE believe what we see.

## Close

I'm going to close this book the way I close all my formal presentations: with a **Challenge** and a **Prediction**.

### *My Challenge*

Craft an Elevator Speech using the templates and Elevator Speech Worksheet.
- Put *your* message out into the world using *your* words.
- Practice it—Tweak it!
- Practice it—Tweak it!
- Practice–Practice–Practice!
- Attend an event where the host says, "Before we get started, let's go around the room and introduce ourselves. Tell us *who* you are and *what* you do. Give us your **Elevator Speech**."

### *My Prediction*

Do *that*, and **my prediction is** *this*:
- You won't panic.
- You won't wish you were elsewhere.

When you stand and speak with confidence in your competence, your Elevator Speech *will* be absolutely, positively,

—no doubt in my mind,

—no ifs, ands, or buts about it,

—*your* mini-presentation will be–*NO SWEAT!*

### *One More Thing*

Steve Jobs, my presentation hero, would often *semi-close* Keynote Presentations with this statement: "One more thing...."

He would then rock the audience by introducing yet another great Apple product or service.

He was the consummate presenter. I've learned a great deal by watching his videos and reading books and articles about his presentation skills.

With the deepest respect and humility, I write, **One More Thing....**

That **One More Thing** is this: I'd like to hear from *you!*

Send me your Elevator Speech!

Visit my blog and post a comment if you're inclined. Whether you agree or disagree, I eagerly await your thoughts.

Feel free to contact me with your questions, suggestions, speaking accomplishments, and, yes, if you have them, *Speaking* **Opportunities!**

**And** *please* **remember:**

"I speak, coach, and write about networking, public speaking, and presentation skills."


Fred E. Miller

**Fred@NoSweatPublicSpeaking.com**

**www.NoSweatPublicSpeaking.com**

# FREE Gifts!

## I have Two FREE Gifts for you!

The **Elevator Speech Template** as a PDF, which goes hand-in-glove with this book.

The **Elevator Speech Worksheet** as a PDF, which has space on each "Floor" to fill in *your* information.

Working with these documents will help you to develop a *great* Elevator Speech with–**NO SWEAT!**

Go here to receive them **FREE:**

**NoSweatPublicSpeaking.com/go/FreeElevatorSpeechTemplate**

## BONUS Gift!

Since you know my mantra is "*Speaking* Opportunities are *Business*, *Career*, and *Leadership* Opportunities!" and an Elevator Speech is a *mini-Speaking* Opportunity, you probably want to start delivering presentations, *correct?* (I hope so!)

To get you started, get my **"Speaker's Template."** This *interactive* PDF visually shows you the structure of an effective presentation. You can use it to develop, practice, and deliver *your* next presentation!

Go here to receive it:

**NoSweatPublicSpeaking.com/Go/Interactive-Speakers-Template/**

Was this book helpful? Then check out Fred Miller's other *NO SWEAT* titles:

## *NO SWEAT Public Speaking!*
*How to Develop, Practice, and Deliver an Incredible Presentation with–NO SWEAT!*

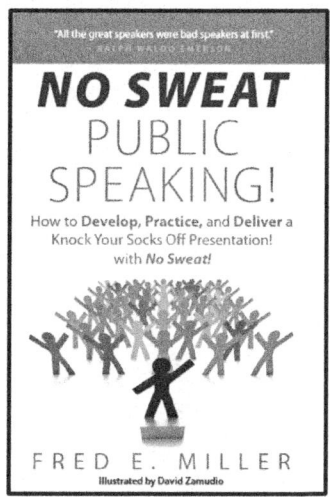

You've Been Asked to Give a Presentation— Is It YES! or YIKES! ?

Have you been asked, or would you like, to:
- Make a Presentation
- Give a Speech
- Give a Toast
- Accept an Award
- Give an Award
- Deliver a Eulogy
- Facilitate a Meeting

PUBLIC SPEAKING is most people's greatest fear. Some fear it more than dying! This fear holds back many people's careers. Like all the skills you possess, this one can also be learned! This book will show you how!

## *The Fear of Public Speaking:*
*Why? & Nuggets to Lessen It with–NO SWEAT!*

Many people find climbing the career ladder, or succeeding in one's own business, usually means doing some speaking in front of groups. It's a credibility builder.

However, because of the Fear of Public Speaking, it's an activity many dread.

It consistently ranks as one of the most common fears people share and holds many back from reaching their potential— personally and professionally.

If you have this fear, or just want to be a better presenter, I have a message for you.

You can find both on Amazon: **Amazon.com/Author/FredEMiller**

Made in United States
North Haven, CT
02 July 2024

54325420R00095